MW00715581

Catalog No. 202042

Published by Pomegranate Communications, Inc.,
Box 6099, Rohnert Park, California 94927

© 2001 Library of Congress

Available in Canada from Canadian Manda Group,
One Atlantic Avenue #105, Toronto, Ontario M6K 3E7, Canada

Available in the U.K. and mainland Europe from Pomegranate Europe Ltd.,
Fullbridge House, Fullbridge, Maldon, Essex CM9 4LE, England

Available in Australia from Hardie Grant Books,
12 Claremont Street, South Yarra, Victoria 3141

Available in New Zealand from Randy Horwood Ltd., P.O. Box 32-077, Devonport, Auckland

Available in Asia (including the Middle East), Africa, and Latin America from
Pomegranate International Sales, 113 Babcombe Drive, Thornhill, Ontario L3T 1M9, Canada

In association with the Library of Congress, Pomegranate also publishes the 2002 wall calendars *Women Who Dare*,
*American Military Aircraft of World War II, The Civil War, Classical Music, Shakespeare's Realm, Edward S. Curtis: Portraits of
Native Americans,* and *David Roberts: Travels in the Holy Land,* as well as the *Today in History* 365-day calendar. Our products
and publications include books, posters, postcards and books of postcards, notecards and boxed notecard sets, magnets,
mousepads, Knowledge Cards™, appointment books and journals, screen savers, and bookmarks.

For more information or to place an order, please contact:
Pomegranate Communications, Inc.
Box 6099, Rohnert Park, California 94927
800-227-1428

Front cover: Annie Smith Peck
American (1850–1935) ■ Mountaineer, Scholar
Prints and Photographs Division ■ LC-USZ62-118273

Cover design by Gina Bostian

All astronomical data supplied in this calendar are expressed in Greenwich Mean Time (GMT).
Moon phases and American, Canadian, and U.K. holidays are noted.

● NEW MOON   ☽ FIRST QUARTER   ○ FULL MOON   ☾ LAST QUARTER

LIBRARY OF CONGRESS   2002 ENGAGEMENT CALENDAR

2002

january

s	m	t	w	t	f	s
		1	2	3	4	5
6	7	8	9	10	11	12
13	14	15	16	17	18	19
20	21	22	23	24	25	26
27	28	29	30	31		

february

s	m	t	w	t	f	s
					1	2
3	4	5	6	7	8	9
10	11	12	13	14	15	16
17	18	19	20	21	22	23
24	25	26	27	28		

march

s	m	t	w	t	f	s
					1	2
3	4	5	6	7	8	9
10	11	12	13	14	15	16
17	18	19	20	21	22	23
24	25	26	27	28	29	30
31						

april

s	m	t	w	t	f	s
	1	2	3	4	5	6
7	8	9	10	11	12	13
14	15	16	17	18	19	20
21	22	23	24	25	26	27
28	29	30				

may

s	m	t	w	t	f	s
			1	2	3	4
5	6	7	8	9	10	11
12	13	14	15	16	17	18
19	20	21	22	23	24	25
26	27	28	29	30	31	

june

s	m	t	w	t	f	s
						1
2	3	4	5	6	7	8
9	10	11	12	13	14	15
16	17	18	19	20	21	22
23	24	25	26	27	28	29
30						

july

s	m	t	w	t	f	s
	1	2	3	4	5	6
7	8	9	10	11	12	13
14	15	16	17	18	19	20
21	22	23	24	25	26	27
28	29	30	31			

august

s	m	t	w	t	f	s
				1	2	3
4	5	6	7	8	9	10
11	12	13	14	15	16	17
18	19	20	21	22	23	24
25	26	27	28	29	30	31

september

s	m	t	w	t	f	s
1	2	3	4	5	6	7
8	9	10	11	12	13	14
15	16	17	18	19	20	21
22	23	24	25	26	27	28
29	30					

october

s	m	t	w	t	f	s
		1	2	3	4	5
6	7	8	9	10	11	12
13	14	15	16	17	18	19
20	21	22	23	24	25	26
27	28	29	30	31		

november

s	m	t	w	t	f	s
					1	2
3	4	5	6	7	8	9
10	11	12	13	14	15	16
17	18	19	20	21	22	23
24	25	26	27	28	29	30

december

s	m	t	w	t	f	s
1	2	3	4	5	6	7
8	9	10	11	12	13	14
15	16	17	18	19	20	21
22	23	24	25	26	27	28
29	30	31				

"Far away there in the sunshine are my highest aspirations," wrote Louisa May Alcott. "I may not reach them, but I can look up and see their beauty, believe in them, and try to follow where they lead." The women featured in this ninth edition of *Women Who Dare*® followed their own aspirations, despite often daunting impediments, and became major achievers in fields ranging from the sciences to the arts, sports to entertainment, exploration to activism. Their lives and accomplishments—and those of many other women from all eras and from countries all around the globe—are celebrated throughout the vast and eclectic collections of the Library of Congress, from which the images and information in this calendar are drawn. We salute these daring adventurers, each of whom found within herself the courage to respond to that disturbing, persistent imperative expressed by American poet Gwendolyn Brooks: "This is the urgency: Live and have your blooming in the noise of the whirlwind."

Text and research by Linda Barrett Osborne, with Athena Angelos, Amy Pastan, and Margaret E. Wagner. Grid entries compiled by Susan Sharp.

Duplicates of images appearing in this calendar, which are accompanied by Library of Congress negative numbers (e.g., LC-USZ62-XXXX), may be ordered from the Library of Congress, Photoduplication Service, Washington, DC 20540-4570; phone: (202) 707-5640; fax: (202) 707-1771.

Dec/Jan

DELIA AKELEY

American (1875–1970)
Explorer, markswoman

Two African elephants stand on display today in Chicago's Field Museum. The smaller, missing a tusk, was shot by taxidermist Carl Akeley; the larger bull, a perfect specimen, by his wife Delia. "I am always frightened in the jungle," this first Western woman to cross the continent of Africa (in 1925) once said, "always prepared for a violent death. But I love it!" Delia made two trips to Africa with Carl to collect museum specimens, and after their divorce she led two further expeditions from Kenya into the Belgian Congo and to the Atlantic Ocean. She traveled by truck, train, camel, and dugout canoe, shot game for display in the Brooklyn Museum, braved fever and a Somali insurrection, and spent several weeks living with Pygmies in Congo's Ituri Forest, recording valuable data on their environment, customs, and society. Back in the U.S., she lectured widely and wrote several books on her travels, including *Jungle Portraits*, an unprecedented collection drawing on 1,500 photos she took of the Pygmies.

Prints and Photographs Division
LC-USZ62-123399

s	m	t	w	t	f	s
		1	2	3	4	5
6	7	8	9	10	11	12
13	14	15	16	17	18	19
20	21	22	23	24	25	26
27	28	29	30	31		

january

Author and home economist Mary Virginia Terhune b. 1831
monday **31** 365

NEW YEAR'S DAY
Betsy Ross b. 1752
tuesday **1** 1

BANK HOLIDAY (SCOTLAND)
M. Carey Thomas, pioneer of women's higher education, b. 1857
wednesday **2** 2

Lucretia Coffin Mott, abolitionist and woman's rights leader, b. 1793
thursday **3** 3

Selena Butler, advocate-leader of interracial cooperation, b. 1872
friday **4** 4

Olympia Brown, pacifist and Universalist minister, b. 1835
saturday **5** 5

Joan of Arc b. 1412
sunday ☾ **6** 6

January

TOSHIKO AKIYOSHI

Japanese/American (b. 1929)
Jazz pianist, bandleader, composer

"Jazz is my music . . . it brings out
my experiences and dreams," said
Toshiko Akiyoshi, whose talent
took her past every barrier in a
musical milieu dominated by
American men. Born to a Japanese
family in Manchuria, Akiyoshi
was an accomplished jazz pianist
in Tokyo when she won a scholar-
ship to study at Boston's Berklee
School of Music. In her early days
in the U.S., she "dealt with both
racial and sexual prejudice. I
played clubs and TV wearing a
kimono, because people were
amazed to see an Oriental woman
playing jazz." Yet Akiyoshi performed with jazz greats like Miles
Davis, Duke Ellington, and Count
Basie, and in 1973 formed the
Toshiko Akiyoshi Jazz Orchestra
with her musician husband to
showcase her own compositions.
Akiyoshi's unique style blends
bebop with Japanese musical
influences. The first woman to
take first place in the *Down Beat*
magazine Reader's Poll as Best
Arranger and Composer, Akiyoshi
has recorded more than fifty
albums and received eleven
Grammy nominations.

New York World-Telegram & Sun
Collection
Prints and Photographs Division
LC-USZ62–125778

s	m	t	w	t	f	s
		1	2	3	4	5
6	7	8	9	10	11	12
13	14	15	16	17	18	19
20	21	22	23	24	25	26
27	28	29	30	31		

january

Marian Anderson debuts at the Metropolitan Opera, 1955

monday
7 7

Ella Grasso is sworn in as first female U.S. governor (of
Connecticut) in her own right, 1975

tuesday
8 8

Carrie Chapman Catt, engineer of "winning plan" that gained
passage of the 19th Amendment (woman suffrage), b. 1859

wednesday
9 9

Katharine Burr Blodgett, developer of the first nonreflecting
glass, b. 1898

thursday
10 10

Amelia Earhart leaves Honolulu on first solo flight across the
Pacific, 1935

friday
11 11

Playwright Lorraine Hansberry, d. 1965

saturday
12 12

Charlotte Ray, first black female lawyer in the U.S., b. 1850

sunday
●**13** 13

January

BYLLYE Y. AVERY
American (b. 1937)
Educator, activist

The recipient of many awards and honors, including a MacArthur Foundation "genius" grant, Byllye Avery is the founding president of the National Black Women's Health Project (NBWHP), headquartered in Atlanta, Georgia. Avery established the NBWHP in 1981 as both a support network and a national forum for the exploration of health issues of African American women. Ten years later it consisted of ninety-six self-help groups in twenty-two states as well as groups in Kenya, Barbados, and Belize. Originally from a background in special education, Avery came gradually to the field of women's health, first cofounding a women's health clinic and then an alternative birthing center in Gainesville, Florida. Today a grassroots network of black female organizations and activism—which NBWHP and Avery have had a significant hand in fostering—continues to grow and make its influence felt. As Avery says, "Our time is coming."

Photograph courtesy National Black Women's Health Project

s	m	t	w	t	f	s
		1	2	3	4	5
6	7	8	9	10	11	12
13	14	15	16	17	18	19
20	21	22	23	24	25	26
27	28	29	30	31		

january

The Massachusetts Colony holds a day of fasting to take "the blame and the shame" for the Salem witch trials and executions, 1697

monday
14 14

MARTIN LUTHER KING JR.'S BIRTHDAY
Jeannette Rankin, age 87, leads 5,000 women in a march on Capitol Hill protesting the Vietnam War, 1968

tuesday
15 15

Writer and thinker Susan Sontag b. 1933

wednesday
16 16

Martha Cotera, Chicana feminist, librarian, and civil rights worker, b. 1938

thursday
17 17

Alice Putnam, kindergarten advocate in the 1870s, b. 1841

friday
18 18

Janis Joplin b. 1943

saturday
19 19

Patricia McCormick becomes the first officially recognized female bullfighter, 1952

sunday
20 20

VALERIE BETTIS

American (1919–1982)
Choreographer, dancer, actress

When Valerie Bettis first started working in film, she was asked what it was like to be successful. "What do you mean?" she replied. "I've always been a success." A modern dance pioneer, Bettis received her early training in her hometown, Houston, Texas, studied in New York, and by age twenty-two was directing her own ensemble. Two years later she choreographed *The Desperate Heart*, a piece hailed as "the finest solo work in the entire modern dance repertory of [its] decade." Bettis created some of her best-known work for other companies: *Virginia Sampler* for the Ballet Russe de Monte Carlo and *A Streetcar Named Desire*, based on the Tennessee Williams play, for the Salvenska-Franklin Ballet. She was often inspired by written works and conveyed a sense of character and temperament in her art. In the 1950s she branched out to choreograph for theater, film, and television and began an acting career. In 1969 she again formed a dance company, and her work continues to be performed today.

New York World-Telegram & Sun
Collection
Prints and Photographs Division
(LC-USZ62–117251)

s	m	t	w	t	f	s
		1	2	3	4	5
6	7	8	9	10	11	12
13	14	15	16	17	18	19
20	21	22	23	24	25	26
27	28	29	30	31		

january

MARTIN LUTHER KING JR. DAY

Sophia Louisa Jex-Blake, English physician who secured the rights of her countrywomen to study and practice medicine, b. 1840

monday
☽ 21
21

Elaine Noble, Massachusetts state legislator and lesbian rights activist, b. 1944

tuesday
22
22

Elizabeth Blackwell becomes the first woman in the U.S. to gain an M.D. degree, 1849

wednesday
23
23

Dr. Mary Edwards Walker receives the Congressional Medal of Honor for her Civil War service, 1866

thursday
24
24

Clarina Nichols, Kansas lecturer on suffrage and abolitionism, b. 1810

friday
25
25

Wu Yi Fang, first and only female college president in China before communism, b. 1893

saturday
26
26

Gospel legend Mahalia Jackson dies in Evergreen Park, Ill., 1972

sunday
27
27

HAZEL BISHOP

American (1906–1998)
Chemist, businesswoman

In 1950 Hazel Bishop's non-smear, kiss-proof "Lasting Lipstick" revolutionized the cosmetic market, but perhaps even more noteworthy was the fact that Bishop was an experienced chemist who created the product after some three hundred experiments in her kitchen. Growing up in an entrepreneurial family in New Jersey, Bishop earned a degree from Barnard College and took graduate classes at Columbia University. She began her career in dermatological research, but throughout the 1940s worked as an organic chemist for oil companies, where she studied and developed aviation fuels, particularly a gasoline for bomber planes. After settling a dispute with the majority stockholder in Hazel Bishop, Inc., the business that launched her lipstick, she founded Hazel Bishop Laboratories to research chemically based, consumer-oriented products. She also set up several companies to manufacture her products, among them an innovative leather cleaner and perfume in a lipstick-like concentrate. In her fifties, the energetic Bishop turned to Wall Street, first becoming a registered agent for a brokerage firm and later a financial analyst.

New York World-Telegram & Sun
    Collection
    Prints and Photographs Division
    (LC-USZ62–125399)

s	m	t	w	t	f	s
					1	2
3	4	5	6	7	8	9
10	11	12	13	14	15	16
17	18	19	20	21	22	23
24	25	26	27	28		

february

Author Colette b. 1873

monday
28   28

Violette Neatley Anderson, first African American woman to practice before the U.S. Supreme Court, b. 1926

tuesday
29   29

Sharon Pratt Kelly, first woman mayor of the District of Columbia, b. 1944

wednesday
30   30

Entertainer Carol Channing b. 1923

thursday
31   31

First U.S. postage stamp to honor an African American woman (Harriet Tubman) is issued, 1978

friday
1   32

Physician Sara Stevenson, first female member of the AMA, b. 1841

saturday
2   33

Jazz pioneer Lil Hardin Armstrong b. 1898

sunday
3   34

February

CLARA BOW

American (1905[6?]–1965)
Actress

"Clara Bow is the quintessence of what the term 'flapper' signifies," pronounced Jazz Age novelist F. Scott Fitzgerald: ". . . pretty, impudent, superbly assured, as worldly-wise, briefly-clad and 'hard-berled' as possible." For 1920s America, Bow was the "It" Girl, symbolizing the assertive, confident, sexually bold new woman who had discarded Victorian values and left the tragedies of World War I behind.

Bow's actual life demanded more courage, complexity, and strength of character than her Hollywood persona. Growing up impoverished in a tenement in Brooklyn, New York, she won a small part in a "Fame and Fortune Contest" held by a movie magazine. Bow made nearly sixty movies in little more than ten years, but retired from the screen at age twenty-six, when her physical and mental health began to deteriorate. Although the tragedies she experienced eventually outpaced her ability to cope, Clara Bow retains an incandescent brightness in the American imagination as a modern woman prepared to shape her own destiny.

Prints and Photographs Division
    LC-USZ62-100842

s	m	t	w	t	f	s
					1	2
3	4	5	6	7	8	9
10	11	12	13	14	15	16
17	18	19	20	21	22	23
24	25	26	27	28		

february

Author Betty Friedan b. 1921

monday
4 35

Mary Gardner, professionalized public health nursing in the U.S. and Europe, b. 1871

tuesday
5 36

Pauline Agassiz Shaw, kindergarten and day-care pioneer, b. 1841

wednesday
6 37

Swiss women gain the right to vote, 1971

thursday
7 38

Elizabeth II is proclaimed queen of England, 1952

friday
8 39

Poet Amy Lowell b. 1874

saturday
9 40

Pioneer electrical engineer Edith Clarke b. 1883

sunday
10 41

GWENDOLYN BROOKS

American (1917–2000)
Poet

"This is the urgency: Live! / and have your blooming / in the noise of the whirlwind," wrote Gwendolyn Brooks, who distilled her experiences as an African American into more than twenty books of poetry. Growing up in Chicago after World War I, in a time of deep-rooted racism and discrimination, Brooks published her first poetry in a local newspaper at age eleven. In 1950 she became the first African American to win the Pulitzer Prize (for "Annie Allen"), and she went on to receive several of literature's most prestigious awards. Brooks dealt honestly and compassionately with difficult themes in her work, including poverty and violence, and she decried ignorance. "I believe that we should all know each other, we human carriers of so many pleasurable differences," she reflected. "To not know is to doubt, to shrink from, sidestep or destroy." She was unremitting in her efforts to teach and to support young writers, and was Illinois' Poet Laureate, as well as poetry consultant (1985–1986) to the Library of Congress.

Library of Congress Photograph
LC-P6-10931-2A

s	m	t	w	t	f	s
					1	2
3	4	5	6	7	8	9
10	11	12	13	14	15	16
17	18	19	20	21	22	23
24	25	26	27	28		

february

Lydia Maria Child, author of influential antislavery works and volumes of advice for women, b. 1802

monday
11 42

LINCOLN'S BIRTHDAY

Juliette Gordon Low establishes the Girl Guides, forerunner of the Girl Scouts of America, 1912

tuesday
12 43

ASH WEDNESDAY

Champion golfer Patty Berg b. 1918

wednesday
13 44

VALENTINE'S DAY

Inventor Margaret E. Knight, who held 27 patents and was called the "female Edison," b. 1838

thursday
14 45

Author Susan Brownmiller b. 1935

friday
15 46

First women's six-day bicycle race ends at Madison Square Garden, New York City, 1889

saturday
16 47

Julia De Burgos, Puerto Rican poet and journalist, b. 1914

sunday
17 48

February

EVELINE BURNS

English/American (1900–1985)
Economist, educator

Every recipient of unemployment insurance and Social Security pension checks owes something to Eveline Burns, one of the leading forces behind the Social Security Act of 1935. Born in London, at age twenty she graduated with honors from the London School of Economics, earning her doctorate in 1926. Two years later she joined the faculty at Columbia University, where she taught in the school of economics, and later the school of social work, for thirty-nine years. Burns once described social policy reform in the 1920s as a job "addressing hundreds of dreary little meetings . . . of long hours . . . composing letters to the press that never got published; or preparing testimony . . . only to find one is allowed to speak less than five minutes." But by 1934, she had become a key player in Franklin Roosevelt's New Deal. Burns went on to direct a federal committee on long-range relief planning, advise the Department of Health, Education and Welfare, develop Columbia's doctoral program in social work, and publish several books and dozens of articles.

New York World-Telegram & Sun Collection
Prints and Photographs Division
LC-USZ62–123842

s	m	t	w	t	f	s
					1	2
3	4	5	6	7	8	9
10	11	12	13	14	15	16
17	18	19	20	21	22	23
24	25	26	27	28		

february

PRESIDENTS' DAY

Author and Nobel laureate Toni Morrison b. 1931

monday
18 49

Short-story writer and novelist Kay Boyle b. 1902

tuesday
19 50

Gloria Vanderbilt, fashion mogul, artist, and actor, b. 1924

wednesday
☽20 51

Barbara Jordan, first congresswoman from the Deep South, b. 1936

thursday
21 52

WASHINGTON'S BIRTHDAY

Sioux activist Gertrude Simmons Bonnin b. 1876

friday
22 53

Fannie Merritt Farmer, author who standardized cooking measurements, b. 1857

saturday
23 54

Author and educator Mary Ellen Chase b. 1887

sunday
24 55

LILLIAN CARTER

American (1898–1983)
Social activist

"Sure I'm for helping the elderly," quipped octogenarian Lillian Carter. "I'm going to be old myself someday." Mother to President Jimmy Carter, Miss Lillian was a remarkable woman in her own right. As a registered nurse in Georgia under legal segregation she made a point of attending to African Americans. After her husband died in 1953, she ran a fraternity house, then a nursing home. At age sixty-eight, she became a Peace Corps volunteer in a village in India, focusing first on education and later on health issues. She steeped herself in Indian culture, attending Hindu discussion groups and learning the Hindi language. Just before her seventieth birthday, Miss Lillian summed up her experience: "I didn't dream that in this remote corner of the world, so far away from the people and material things that I had always considered so necessary, I would discover what Life is really all about. Sharing yourself with others, and accepting their love for you, is the most precious gift of all."

Prints and Photographs Division
   LC-USZ62-93591

s	m	t	w	t	f	s
					1	2
3	4	5	6	7	8	9
10	11	12	13	14	15	16
17	18	19	20	21	22	23
24	25	26	27	28	29	30
31						

march

PURIM (BEGINS AT SUNSET)
Nutrition writer Adelle Davis b. 1904

monday
25   56

Sue S. Dauser is appointed first female captain in the U.S. Navy, 1944

tuesday
26   57

Actor and AIDS activist Elizabeth Taylor b. 1932

wednesday
27   58

Actor and singer Bernadette Peters b. 1948

thursday
28   59

Rebecca Lee of Boston, Mass., becomes the first African American woman to gain a medical degree, 1864

friday
1   60

Women begin pilot training for the U.S. Navy, 1973

saturday
2   61

Track star and Olympic medalist Jackie Joyner-Kersee b. 1962

sunday
3   62

DIANA CHANG
Chinese/American (b. 192?)
Writer, painter, teacher

When Diana Chang published *The Frontiers of Love* in 1956, she was marking out relatively new territory for the novel. Her story of Eurasians in Shanghai, Westernized despite their ties to China, explored the issue of national and racial identity long before "diversity" and "multiculturalism" became common terms. Chang's perspective was forged from her own experiences as the child of a Chinese father and Eurasian mother. She was born in New York City, but grew up in Beijing and Shanghai, returning to the U.S. at the end of World War II to study at Barnard College. She is the author of five additional novels and three volumes of poetry, an accomplished painter, and she has inspired a younger generation through her teaching at Barnard. "I didn't want to spend, so much as I wanted to build. I wanted to live my life, without any concessions made, one full day after another," the narrator concludes Chang's second novel, words that aptly apply to Chang herself.

New York World-Telegram & Sun Collection
Prints and Photographs Division
LC-USZ62–116103

s	m	t	w	t	f	s
					1	2
3	4	5	6	7	8	9
10	11	12	13	14	15	16
17	18	19	20	21	22	23
24	25	26	27	28	29	30
31						

march

Jeannette Rankin of Montana is sworn in as the first female member of Congress, 1917

monday
4   63

Lady Isabella Gregory, Irish playwright and founder of the Abbey Theatre, b. 1852

tuesday
5   64

Eleanor Roosevelt becomes the first First Lady to travel by air to a foreign country, 1934

wednesday
6   65

Joyce Steele and Jessie Cooper are the first women to be elected to the South Australian Parliament, 1959

thursday
7   66

Jockey Barbara Jo Rubin b. 1969

friday
8   67

English actor Glenda Jackson b. 1936

saturday
9   68

MOTHERING SUNDAY (U.K.)
Women's rights activist Hallie Quinn Brown b. 1845

sunday
10   69

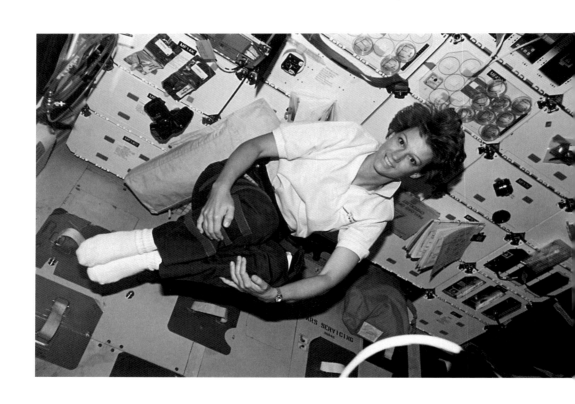

EILEEN COLLINS

American (b. 1956)
Astronaut

NASA mission STS-93 was the culmination of a dream for astronaut Eileen Collins. As the forty-two-year-old pilot safely landed the space shuttle *Columbia* at Cape Canaveral, Florida, on July 27, 1999, she made history as NASA's first female shuttle commander. Her successful five-day mission, in which the $1.5 billion Chandra X-ray telescope was launched into orbit, prompted Vice President Al Gore to declare that she had "not only equaled but surpassed Amelia Earhart in the history of flight." Indeed Earhart, who attempted to become the first woman aviator to fly around the world, is one of Collins' heroes. Collins read voraciously about the feats of women aviators in high school and by 1977 had earned a pilot's license. After graduating from Syracuse University in 1978, she entered Air Force pilot training. In February 1995, she became the first woman to pilot a shuttle mission. The mother of a young daughter, Collins credits her success to "the accomplishments of women who came before me."

Courtesy of NASA

s	m	t	w	t	f	s
					1	2
3	4	5	6	7	8	9
10	11	12	13	14	15	16
17	18	19	20	21	22	23
24	25	26	27	28	29	30
31						

march

Mme. d'Epinay, author who won fame with her *Conversations of Emily* and *Memoirs and Correspondence*, b. 1726

monday
11 70

Annette Adams, first female federal prosecutor, b. 1877

tuesday
12 71

Susan B. Anthony dies at age 86, leaving her $10,000 estate to the cause of woman suffrage, 1906

wednesday
13 72

Lucy Hobbs Taylor, first woman to obtain a dental degree in the U.S., b. 1833

thursday
●**14** 73

Margaret Webster, first female director at the Metropolitan Opera House in New York City, b. 1905

friday
15 74

Aviator Margie Hurley becomes the first woman to break the 300 m.p.h. airspeed barrier, 1947

saturday
16 75

ST. PATRICK'S DAY
Artist and illustrator Kate Greenaway b. 1846

sunday
17 76

March

MAUREEN CONNOLLY
American (1934–1969)
Athlete

In just four years before a horse-back riding accident ended her competitive career at age nineteen, Maureen Connolly—dubbed Little Mo by the media—had already become the dominant force in international tennis and one of the top players of all time. Combining natural talent with hard work even as a child, Connolly won more than fifty junior titles with only four defeats, and was the youngest person to win the national junior title. The first woman to win tennis's Grand Slam—Wimbledon and the U.S., French, and Australian championships—Connolly racked up victory after victory with precision baseline drives and formidable ground strokes. She was known for her intense concentration on the court and for the ability to intimidate opponents with a poker face and businesslike, even cold manner. Yet she was generous to young players, coaching after she could no longer play, and she founded the Maureen Connolly Brinker Foundation six months before her untimely death from cancer.

New York World-Telegram & Sun
   Collection
   Prints and Photographs Division
   LC-USZ62–115338

s	m	t	w	t	f	s
					1	2
3	4	5	6	7	8	9
10	11	12	13	14	15	16
17	18	19	20	21	22	23
24	25	26	27	28	29	30
31

march

BANK HOLIDAY (N. IRELAND)
Speed-skating champ Bonnie Blair b. 1964

monday
18

Comedian "Moms" Mabley b. 1897

tuesday
19 78

VERNAL EQUINOX 7:16 P.M. (GMT)
Yoko Ono marries John Lennon, 1969

wednesday
20 79

Debi Thomas becomes the first African American woman to win the gold medal in a world skating competition, 1986

thursday
21 80

Poet Phyllis McGinley b. 1905

friday
☽ **22** 81

Virginia and Leonard Woolf establish the Hogarth Press, 1917

saturday
23 82

PALM SUNDAY
Dorothy Stratton, director of the U.S. Coast Guard Women (SPARS) during World War II, b. 1899

sunday
24 83

ISADORA DUNCAN

American (1878–1927)
Dancer, choreographer

A budding dance instructor from the age of six, by her early teens Isadora Duncan had some of San Francisco's wealthiest families among her clientele. With a combination of natural grace and chutzpah, she taught "any pretty thing that came into my head." As her talent matured, her creative energy was increasingly devoted to what would be her life's mission—the search for a means of expressive dance outside the strictures of classical ballet. Undaunted by troupe work and unappreciative producers in New York and wanting recognition, Duncan moved to Paris in 1900. She was soon appearing throughout Europe before large and ecstatic crowds who were stunned by her power and originality as a performer. "The divine, the holy Isadora" led a life marked by artistic triumph, fame, controversy, and tragedy, most of it inimitably recounted in her autobiography *My Life*. A pivotal figure in the history of dance, Duncan inspired millions with her pioneering achievements and refusal to conform to prevailing codes of female dress or conduct.

Prints and Photographs Division
LC-G432-0958-N

s	m	t	w	t	f	s
					1	2
3	4	5	6	7	8	9
10	11	12	13	14	15	16
17	18	19	20	21	22	23
24	25	26	27	28	29	30
31						

march

Japanese poet and novelist Higuchi Ichiyo (*Growing Up*, 1895) b. 1872

monday
25 84

Louise Otto, German author and feminist pioneer, b. 1819

tuesday
26 85

FIRST NIGHT OF PASSOVER
Ruth Hanna McCormick, newspaper publisher and U.S. congresswoman, b. 1880

wednesday
27 86

SECOND NIGHT OF PASSOVER
St. Teresa of Avila, influential mystic and author, b. 1515

thursday
28 87

GOOD FRIDAY
Author Judith Guest (*Ordinary People*), b. 1936

friday
29 88

Pioneer psychologist Melanie Klein b. 1882

saturday
30 89

EASTER SUNDAY
SUMMER TIME BEGINS (U.K.)

sunday
31 90

Abigail Adams writes to husband John, who is helping frame the Declaration of Independence: "Remember the ladies . . . [we] will not hold ourselves bound by any Laws in which we have no voice." (1776)

April

MILLICENT FENWICK

American (1910–1992)
Congresswoman, diplomat, editor

When New Jersey state legislator
Millicent Fenwick was campaigning
for ratification of the Equal Rights
Amendment, a fellow assemblyman
announced that he preferred
women to be kissable, cuddly, and
to smell good. "That's exactly how
I like my men," Fenwick told him,
"and I do hope you haven't been
disappointed as often as I have."
Known for her strong convictions,
honesty and distinctive style—the
pipe-smoking Fenwick was the
model for the *Doonesbury* cartoon's
Lacey Davenport—she transformed
a privileged background into a
life of public service. The one-time
Vogue model and editor (she wrote
the 1948 *Vogue's Book of Etiquette*)
also served on a New Jersey school
board and as director of the state's
consumer affairs. In 1974 she successfully ran for Congress as the
Republican candidate, serving
four terms. Fenwick supported
food stamps and federal funding
for abortion, and was instrumental
in establishing the Helsinki
Commission on Human Rights.
From 1983 to 1987 she was the U.S.
ambassador to the United Nations
Agencies for Food and Agriculture.

Prints and Photographs Division
    LC-USZ62–122204

s	m	t	w	t	f	s
	1	2	3	4	5	6
7	8	9	10	11	12	13
14	15	16	17	18	19	20
21	22	23	24	25	26	27
28	29	30				

april

EASTER MONDAY (CANADA, U.K.)   *monday*
Wangari Maathai, Kenyan human rights and environmental
activist, b. 1940

1   91

Feminist scholar Barbara Caine (*Victorian Feminists*), b. 1948   *tuesday*

2   92

Animal behaviorist Jane Goodall b. 1934   *wednesday*

3   93

Author, actor, and journalist Maya Angelou b. 1928   *thursday*

☽ **4**   94

Catherine I, empress of Russia, b. 1684   *friday*

5   95

Labor leader Rose Schneiderman b. 1884   *saturday*

6   96

DAYLIGHT SAVING TIME BEGINS   *sunday*
Everglades conservation activist Marjory Stoneman Douglas
b. 1890

7   97

April

ANNA FREUD
Austrian/English (1895–1982)
Psychoanalyst

Sigmund Freud had six children, but it was only his youngest, a daughter, who carried on his legacy of inquiry into the mind and made her own significant contributions to psychology. Anna Freud was already reading her father's work at age fourteen. In 1918 she began psychoanalysis with him, and in 1922 she became a member of the Vienna Psychoanalytic Society. Anna devoted her career to applying psychoanalytic techniques and theories to children and adolescents. She remained true to her father's basic teachings, but her best-known work, *The Ego and the Mechanisms of Defense* (1935), went beyond Freud's theories to incorporate what she had learned from experience, dealing with social and developmental issues. After emigrating to England on the eve of World War II, she established the Hampstead War Nursery, which evolved into the Hampstead Clinic, directed by Anna after 1952. She continued to write, travel, and lecture—delving into everything from transference symptoms in child analysis to crime and the family—until her death.

Prints and Photographs Division
LC-USZ62-98478

s	m	t	w	t	f	s
	1	2	3	4	5	6
7	8	9	10	11	12	13
14	15	16	17	18	19	20
21	22	23	24	25	26	27
28	29	30				

april

Sonja Henie, world champion figure skater for ten consecutive years, b. 1913

monday
8 98

Marie Luhring, first woman in the Society of Automotive Engineers, b. 1920

tuesday
9 99

Women are first ordained as pastors in Sweden's Evangelical Lutheran Church, 1960

wednesday
10 100

Columnist Ellen Goodman b. 1941

thursday
11 101

Criminologist Eleanor Touroff Glueck b. 1883

friday
● **12** 102

Eudora Welty, the only living author (thus far) to have e-mail software named after her, b. 1909

saturday
13 103

Anne Mansfield Sullivan, teacher of Helen Keller, b. 1866

sunday
14 104

April

FRIEDA HENNOCK

Polish/American (1904–1960)
Attorney, FCC commissioner

Dubbed "the most controversial figure" on the Federal Communications Commission by NBC TV's *Meet the Press*, Frieda Hennock was the first woman appointed to the FCC (in 1948) or to any federal regulatory agency. Hennock won her reputation by challenging the commercial broadcast industry and her six male FCC colleagues to reserve channels for educational television stations. An experienced attorney who had practiced law for twenty-two years in New York City, where her Polish family immigrated in 1910, Hennock threw herself into mastering the technical and policy aspects of the communications industries. She became a voice for women's interests, but she was also concerned with the wider ramifications of television, which, she pointed out, entered the "homes . . . of adults and children . . . [giving] them information on the widest scale. Through [it] we are influenced in . . . our thinking, in our manners, and our morals." She almost singlehandedly campaigned for educational programming through hearings, media broadcasts and speaking appearances, securing 252 educational channels before she left the FCC in 1955.

s	m	t	w	t	f	s
	1	2	3	4	5	6
7	8	9	10	11	12	13
14	15	16	17	18	19	20
21	22	23	24	25	26	27
28	29	30				

april

Vigdis Finnbogadottir, president of Iceland, b. 1930

monday
15

Beverly Kelley becomes the first female commander of a Coast Guard ship, 1979

tuesday
16 106

Editor and pioneer penologist Isabel Barrows b. 1845

wednesday
17 107

Women's World Fair opens in Chicago, 1925

thursday
18 108

Diarist and businesswoman Sarah Kemble Knight b. 1666

friday
19 109

New Zealand–born American Helen Thayer, traveling on foot and on skis, reaches the North Pole with her sole companion, a husky, 1988

saturday
☽ **20** 110

Author, professor of theology, and Methodist pastor Rev. Dr. Georgia Elma Harkness b. 1891

sunday
21 111

April

BEATRICE HICKS

American (1919–1979)
Engineer

Receiving little encouragement to become an engineer in the 1930s— even from her father, an engineering executive—Beatrice Hicks nonetheless earned four degrees in engineering and physics, daring to succeed in what she called "a man's world." After a stint as the first woman engineer at Western Electric, Hicks joined her father's company, serving as chief engineer and later as president. She was among the first to work on developing and manufacturing pressure and gas density controls for airplanes and missiles, and invented the gas density switch used in extreme atmospheric conditions. In 1950 she was a founder and first president of the Society of Women Engineers, making recruitment of young women to the field a top priority. She observed that in 1951 only seventy-seven of 105,000 women graduated from college with a specialty in engineering. "Almost this entire [group] have never been . . . advised that engineering is a profession open to them," said Hicks, whose career belied the conventional notion of a suitable job for a woman.

s	m	t	w	t	f	s
	1	2	3	4	5	6
7	8	9	10	11	12	13
4	15	16	17	18	19	20
21	22	23	24	25	26	27
8	29	30				

april

EARTH DAY

Rita Levi-Montalcini, Italian neurobiologist and Nobel laureate, b. 1909

monday
22   112

Dame Edith Ngaio Marsh, one of New Zealand's most popular authors, creator of Scotland Yard inspector Roderick Alleyn, b. 1899

tuesday
23   113

Singer, actor, and director Barbra Streisand b. 1942

wednesday
24   114

Jazz great Ella Fitzgerald b. 1918

thursday
25   115

Sixteen-year-old Sybil Ludington rides through towns in New York and Connecticut warning citizens of advancing British troops and amassing resistance, 1777

friday
26   116

British aviator Sheila Scott, author of *I Must Fly*, b. 1927

saturday
27   117

Singer and pianist Blossom Dearie b. 1926

sunday
28   118

386

Apr/May

MARGUERITE HIGGINS

American (1920–1966)
War correspondent/author

The "front is no place for a woman to be running around," declared General Walton Walker when he banned female reporters from covering the Korean War. But Marguerite Higgins told General Douglas MacArthur that she was a journalist, not a woman, and she stayed. "I have known since childhood that if there was to be a war I wanted to be there to know for myself what force cuts so deep into the hearts of men," Higgins wrote in her autobiography. During World War II, she was with the Allied forces when they opened the Nazi concentration camps at Buchenwald and Dachau. In Korea, she landed with the U.S. Marines behind North Korean lines; in 1951 she won the Pulitzer Prize for foreign correspondence. Higgins wrote several books, including *Our Vietnam Nightmare* (1965), which criticized American policy based on her firsthand observations of the conflict there since 1953. She died at age forty-five of a tropical disease she contracted while reporting in Vietnam.

New York World-Telegram & Sun
Collection
Prints and Photographs Division
LC-USZ62–111601

s	m	t	w	t	f	s
			1	2	3	4
5	6	7	8	9	10	11
12	13	14	15	16	17	18
19	20	21	22	23	24	25
26	27	28	29	30	31	

may

Florence Sabin becomes the first woman elected to the National Academy of Sciences, 1925

monday
29 119

Actor Eve Arden, "Our Miss Brooks," b. 1912

tuesday
30 120

Gwendolyn Brooks becomes first African American woman to win the Pulitzer Prize in poetry, 1950

wednesday
1 121

Catherine II ("the Great") of Russia, one of the most influential rulers in Western history, b. 1729

thursday
2 122

Belva Lockwood, after successfully lobbying Congress to end gender apartheid at the bar of the U.S. Supreme Court, becomes the first woman to argue before that court, 1879

friday
3 123

Anna Chandy, first female judge in India, b. 1905

saturday
4 124

CINCO DE MAYO

Dr. Dorothy H. Andersen identifies the disease cystic fibrosis, 1938

sunday
5 125

VINNIE REAM HOXIE

American (1847–1914)
Sculptor

In 1864, Abraham Lincoln agreed to pose for a portrait bust to be created by a diminutive, curly-haired, seventeen-year-old Post Office clerk, Vinnie Ream Hoxie. After his death, Congress awarded her a $10,000 contract for a full-length, standing statue of Lincoln to be placed in the Capitol rotunda, making her the first woman commissioned to execute a sculpture for the U.S. government. The remarkable Hoxie had the ability to sculpt in clay, marble, and later, bronze, with almost no formal training. Before she was twenty-one, she had sculpted the likes of General George Custer, Radical Republican Thaddeus Stevens, and Horace Greeley, and won the support of the powerful and influential of the nation's capital. In Europe, where she completed her Lincoln statue, she charmed society with her independent spirit, determination, and energy. One of her best known works is a statue of Admiral David G. Farragut, which still stands in Washington, D.C.'s Farragut Square. Her Lincoln also remains in Washington, along with two other sculptures in Statuary Hall at the Capitol.

Prints and Photographs Division
LC-USZ62-10284

s	m	t	w	t	f	s
			1	2	3	4
5	6	7	8	9	10	11
12	13	14	15	16	17	18
19	20	21	22	23	24	25
26	27	28	29	30	31	

may

BANK HOLIDAY (U.K.)   *monday*
Phebe Hanaford, author and Universalist minister, b. 1829
6   126

Ruth Prawer Jhabvala, Anglo-Indian author and screenwriter, b. 1927   *tuesday*
7   127

Mary Lou Williams, "first lady of jazz," b. 1910   *wednesday*
8   128

Journalist, author, and musician Philippa Duke Schuyler dies in a helicopter crash in Vietnam, 1967   *thursday*
9   129

Dancer and choreographer Judith Jameson b. 1944   *friday*
10   130

Dancer and choreographer Martha Graham b. 1893   *saturday*
11   131

MOTHER'S DAY   *sunday*
Sharon S. Adams leaves Yokohama, Japan, on first solo transpacific crossing by a woman, 1969   ●**12**   132

RUBY HURLEY

American (b. c. 1913)
Civil rights activist

In 1951 Ruby Hurley arrived in Birmingham, Alabama, to open the first permanent office of the National Association for the Advancement of Colored People in the deep South. The first professional civil rights worker in the South encountered rigid segregation—"Negroes and whites could not play checkers together," she once recalled. Hurley had begun her career with the NAACP in 1939 when she organized a youth council in Washington, D.C. In 1943, she became the national youth secretary. After she moved to Birmingham, she daily placed her life at risk by investigating the lynching of several African Americans and by supporting Autherine Lucy in her bid to enter the all-white University of Alabama. As a result, "I could be riding down the street and white men would drive by and say, 'We gon' get you,'" said Hurley. ". . . Bombs were thrown at my home." In 1956, when the state of Alabama closed down the NAACP office, Hurley went to Atlanta, where she continued the struggle for civil rights.

New York World-Telegram & Sun
Collection
Prints and Photographs Division
LC-USZ62–111237

s	m	t	w	t	f	s
			1	2	3	4
5	6	7	8	9	10	11
12	13	14	15	16	17	18
19	20	21	22	23	24	25
26	27	28	29	30	31	

may

Author Daphne du Maurier b. 1907

monday
13 133

Mary Williams, who helped resolve boundary disputes between Honduras, Guatemala, and Nicaragua, b. 1878

tuesday
14 134

Mary Kies becomes first U.S. woman granted a patent (for "a new and useful improvement in weaving straw with silk or thread"), 1809

wednesday
15 135

Anthropologist Mary Thygeson Shepardson b. 1906

thursday
16 136

U.S. Energy Secretary Hazel O'Leary b. 1937

friday
17 137

ARMED FORCES DAY
Aviator Jackie Cochran breaks the sound barrier, 1953

saturday
18 138

Australian soprano Dame Nellie Melba b. 1861

sunday
☽**19** 139

May

JUNE JORDAN
American (b. 1936)
Author

"What has been called 'women's work' traditionally includes the nurturing of young people, maintaining a house, providing the wherewithal so that people can keep going . . . My work is closely related in purpose to the traditional work." Poetry (*Things I Do in the Dark*), essays (*Civil Wars*), articles, and works for and about children (*The Voice of the Children*) are some elements of the work Jordan has chosen. Born black in a society in which "a white stare" often dismissed her realities and entranced from youth with the "possibility of language, of writing, [which] seemed to me magical and basic and irresistible," Jordan embraced the profession of writing, believing that "by declaring the truth, you create the truth." Her blunt, caustically eloquent declarations explore, expose, criticize, and propose avenues of expression for "the living Black experience": "I will not walk politely on the pavements anymore / and this is dedicated in particular / to those who hear my footsteps . . . / then turn around / see me / and hurry on."

Manuscript Division

s	m	t	w	t	f	s
			1	2	3	4
5	6	7	8	9	10	11
12	13	14	15	16	17	18
19	20	21	22	23	24	25
26	27	28	29	30	31	

may

VICTORIA DAY (CANADA)
Norwegian novelist Sigrid Undset (1928 Nobel laureate in literature) b. 1882

monday
20 140

Frances Densmore, ethnomusicologist who recorded songs of Native Americans, b. 1867

tuesday
21 141

Impressionist painter Mary Cassatt b. 1844

wednesday
22 142

Margaret Fuller, intellectual extraordinaire of the nineteenth century, b. 1810

thursday
23 143

Helen Taussig, physician who diagnosed the cause of "blue babies," b. 1898

friday
24 144

Mme. C. J. Walker, first self-made female millionaire in U.S., d. 1919

saturday
25 145

Sally Ride, physicist and first U.S. woman in space, b. 1951

sunday
○ **26** 146

FRANCES KELLOR

American (1873–1952)
Reformer

Motivated by compassion and patriotism, Frances Kellor was a leading advocate of the Americanization Movement in the early twentieth century, working to aid immigrants and to quickly assimilate them into American society. Forced to leave high school for financial reasons, Kellor developed a growing awareness of social issues. She passed a special exam to attend law school at Cornell and studied at the University of Chicago, where she lived in Jane Addams' Hull House, in daily contact with new arrivals to this country. Working through New York state agencies, she campaigned against overcrowded, unsanitary living conditions and championed the rights of both immigrants and African American migrant workers from the South. Kellor combatted nativist sentiments by aggressively promoting naturalization. She organized English classes, encouraged citizenship and cultural education, and orchestrated a National Americanization Day in 1915 in which tens of thousands of immigrants in 150 cities took part. After immigration declined in the 1920s, Kellor devoted herself to international arbitration for the last twenty-five years of her life.

Prints and Photographs Division
   LC-USZ62-99077

s	m	t	w	t	f	s
						1
2	3	4	5	6	7	8
9	10	11	12	13	14	15
6	17	18	19	20	21	22
3	24	25	26	27	28	29
0						

june

MEMORIAL DAY OBSERVED
BANK HOLIDAY (U.K.)
Biologist and author Rachel Carson b. 1907

monday
27   147

Poet May Swenson b. 1919

tuesday
28   148

Elizabeth Pringle, South Carolina plantation owner and author, b. 1845

wednesday
29   149

MEMORIAL DAY
Astronomer Maria Mitchell becomes the first woman elected to the American Academy of Arts and Sciences, 1848

thursday
30   150

Mary Hannah Fulton, founder of the Hackett Medical College for Women in Canton, China, b. 1854

friday
31   151

Mme. Adolphe becomes the first woman to perform on a tightrope in the U.S., New York City, 1819

saturday
1   152

African American novelist Dorothy West b. 1907

sunday
2   153

Wanda Landowska

Polish (1877–1959)
Musician, teacher

A brilliant harpsichord performer of Bach, Couperin, and Handel, Wanda Landowska virtually reinvented the playing of seventeenth- and eighteenth-century music in the first part of the twentieth century. Determined to provide authenticity in performance, Landowska researched the variety of harpsichords on which this music was meant to be performed, as well as its original style. She astonished audiences with her vivid interpretations, bringing to life the music's subtlety and lively charm. She also wrote several invaluable books on Baroque music. Landowska—who even as a child prodigy in her native Warsaw was fascinated by music of an earlier time—moved to Paris in 1900. She founded the École de Musique Ancienne, a renowned study and concert center and repository of ancient instruments, books, and manuscripts. Landowska was forced to abandon these because of her Jewish heritage when the Nazis invaded France. She settled in the United States and continued to give virtuoso performances on the harpsichord and piano.

s	m	t	w	t	f	s
						1
2	3	4	5	6	7	8
9	10	11	12	13	14	15
16	17	18	19	20	21	22
23	24	25	26	27	28	29
30						

june

Entertainer and activist Josephine Baker b. 1906

monday
3 154

Carson McCullers, age 23, publishes *The Heart Is a Lonely Hunter* to critical acclaim, 1940

tuesday
4 155

Native Hawaiian feminist Kaahumanu d. 1832

wednesday
5 156

Marian Wright Edelman, founder of the Children's Defense Fund, b. 1939

thursday
6 157

Writer and activist Nikki Giovanni b. 1943

friday
7 158

Mystery writer Sara Paretsky b. 1947

saturday
8 159

Georgia Neese Clark is confirmed as first female treasurer of the U.S., 1949

sunday
9 160

EVA LE GALLIENNE

American (1899–1991)
Actress, director, producer, author

She played Juliet, Hedda Gabler, and Queen Elizabeth to rave notices, but for some seventy years, Eva Le Galliene was as famous for her work off stage as on it. She broke new ground in the American theater by founding and directing repertory companies to perform classical drama at reasonable prices, the precursor of today's off-Broadway–style productions. Le Gallienne brought the plays of Chekov, Shakespeare, and Ibsen— whom she also translated into English—as well as distinguished contemporary drama to a wide audience. While on tour with her Civic Repertory Theater (1926–1933), she contrasted her efforts with commercial theater and spoke of "returning [theater] into the hands of the workers . . . who have the training, knowledge and integrity to serve it well." Among many honors, Le Gallienne received the National Medal of the Arts, and an Oscar nomination for her performance in the 1980 film *Resurrection.* At age eighty-three she played the White Queen in *Alice in Wonderland,* a work she had adapted and starred in fifty years before.

New York World-Telegram & Sun
Collection
Prints and Photographs Division
LC-USZ62-113316

s	m	t	w	t	f	s
						1
2	3	4	5	6	7	8
9	10	11	12	13	14	15
6	17	18	19	20	21	22
3	24	25	26	27	28	29
0						

june

Bridget Bishop becomes the first of the Salem "witches" to be hanged, 1692

monday
10 161

English photographer Julia Margaret Cameron b. 1815

tuesday
11 162

Babe Didrikson Zaharias becomes the first U.S. woman to win the British Women's Amateur Golf Tournament, 1947

wednesday
12 163

Mystery writer and classicist Dorothy L. Sayers b. 1893

thursday
13 164

FLAG DAY
Photojournalist Margaret Bourke-White b. 1906

friday
14 165

Malvina Hoffman, sculptor who created 110 life-size figures for the Field Museum of Chicago, b. 1887

saturday
15 166

FATHER'S DAY
Junko Tabei becomes the first woman to reach the summit of Mt. Everest, 1975

sunday
16 167

LILLIAN LEITZEL

German (1882–1931)
Aerialist

Spinning through the air with the greatest of ease, the daring and adorable young woman on the turning trapeze was Lillian Leitzel. At four feet nine inches tall and weighing ninety-five pounds, the "Queen of the Aerialists" once said, "I'd rather be a racehorse and last a minute than be a plowhorse and last forever." Leitzel was born in Breslau, Germany, to a family of popular trapeze artists. At nine years old, she had built her own trapeze and begun to train, becoming part of the family act for several seasons. In 1915 she joined the Ringling Brothers Circus in the U.S., and by 1919, when they merged with Barnum and Bailey, Leitzel commanded a high salary and her own Pullman car. Her bold signature act, the one-armed plunge or "swing over," astonished crowds everywhere. Her record was 249 rotations in one performance. Still performing at age fifty-five, Leitzel died from injuries sustained in a fall: the metal in her swivel ring had crystallized, causing it to break.

New York World-Telegram & Sun
Collection
Prints and Photographs Division
LC-USZ62-122867

s	m	t	w	t	f	s
						1
2	3	4	5	6	7	8
9	10	11	12	13	14	15
16	17	18	19	20	21	22
23	24	25	26	27	28	29
30						

june

Susan La Flesche Picotte, Omaha Indian physician, b. 1865

monday
17 168

Susan B. Anthony, fined $100 for "illegal voting," informs the judge she will never pay it (she never did), 1873

tuesday
☽ **18** 169

Aung San Suu Kyi, Burmese human rights leader and Nobel Peace Prize laureate, b. 1945

wednesday
19 170

Queen Victoria of England begins her 64-year reign, 1837

thursday
20 171

SUMMER SOLSTICE 1:24 P.M.(GMT)
Novelist and dramatist Françoise Sagan (*Bonjour Tristesse*) b. 1935

friday
21 172

Alice Gertrude Bryand and Florence West Duckering become the first women admitted to the American College of Surgeons, 1914

saturday
22 173

Russian poet Anna Akhmatova b. 1889

sunday
23 174

June

EDMONIA LEWIS

American (1843?–after 1911)
Sculptor

Edmonia Lewis, who declared her strong sympathy for "all women who have struggled and suffered," created idealized sculptures based on themes from her personal heritage. Born to a Chippewa mother and an African American father near Albany, New York, she spent her childhood years traveling with her mother's tribe. She was orphaned as a teenager but managed, with the financial help of a brother, to enter Oberlin College. Despite the strong abolitionist presence there, Lewis encountered searing prejudice. She was determined to pursue a career, however, and moved to Boston, where the fine examples of public sculpture inspired her to study art. In 1865, following several other expatriate women artists, Lewis settled in Rome. She produced ambitious works, including *Forever Free*, which depicts a black man and woman breaking the chains of bondage, and *Old Arrow Maker*, which glorified the industrious lives of Native Americans. With the exhibition of her monumental *Cleopatra* at the Philadelphia Centennial Exposition in 1876, she secured her place as one of the first African American sculptors to receive international recognition.

Publishing Office

s	m	t	w	t	f	s
						1
2	3	4	5	6	7	8
9	10	11	12	13	14	15
16	17	18	19	20	21	22
23	24	25	26	27	28	29
30						

june

American novelist Rebecca Blaine Harding Davis, mother and fiercest critic of journalist and novelist Richard Harding Davis, b. 1831
monday 24 175

Carly Simon, singer and composer, b. 1945
tuesday 25 176

Pearl Buck, winner of the 1938 Nobel Prize in literature, b. 1892
wednesday 26 177

Antoinette Perry, founder of the American Theater Wing, person for whom the Tony Awards are named, b. 1888
thursday 27 178

Molly Pitcher takes the place of her wounded husband in the Battle of Monmouth, 1778
friday 28 179

Journalist Oriana Fallaci b. 1930
saturday 29 180

Entertainer Lena Horne b. 1917
sunday 30 181

July

SOPHIE IRENE LOEB

American (1876–1929)
Social activist, journalist

Daughter of a widowed Russian
immigrant mother, Sophie Irene
Loeb knew firsthand the plight of
women and children deprived of a
father's income, and she had the
courage and vision to crusade for
assistance to impoverished families
throughout her life. After leaving
school, Loeb taught and wrote for
a Pittsburgh newspaper to support
her mother and younger siblings.
In 1910 she moved to New York,
where, as a reporter for the *Evening
World*, she wrote a series of articles
on slum children that led to the
formation of the New York State
Commission on Relief for Widowed
Mothers and eventual legislation
providing them with financial aid.
Loeb headed the New York Child
Welfare Board, without pay, for
seven years, at the same time
campaigning for better housing,
maternity care, and decent education for tenement dwellers. She
cofounded and served as president
of the Child Welfare Commission
of America, drawing national
attention to her concerns, and
was a child welfare advisor to the
League of Nations.

New York World-Telegram & Sun
    Collection
    Prints and Photographs Division
    LC-USZ62–116626

s	m	t	w	t	f	s
	1	2	3	4	5	6
7	8	9	10	11	12	13
4	15	16	17	18	19	20
1	22	23	24	25	26	27
8	29	30	31			

july

CANADA DAY (CANADA)
Choreographer Twyla Tharp b. 1942

monday
1 182

Amelia Earhart loses radio contact in the Pacific, 1937

tuesday
2 183

Maria Martin, the only woman among naturalist John James
Audubon's three assistants, b. 1796

wednesday
3 184

INDEPENDENCE DAY
English actor Gertrude Lawrence, b. 1901

thursday
4 185

Juanita M. Kreps becomes the first female governor of the New
York Stock Exchange, 1972

friday
5 186

English children's writer and illustrator Beatrix Potter b. 1866

saturday
6 187

Martina Navratilova wins her third straight Wimbledon singles
crown, 1984

sunday
7 188

Alice Roosevelt Longworth
American (1884–1980)
Society leader, wit

"If you haven't got anything nice to say about somebody, come sit next to me," quipped Alice Roosevelt Longworth, daughter of Theodore Roosevelt, who was known to comment that he could govern the country or govern his impossibly headstrong daughter, but he couldn't do both. Married to Congressman (later Speaker of the House) Nicholas Longworth in 1906, Alice Longworth wielded tremendous political influence with both her verbal barbs and her powerful political connections. Ever independent, in 1912 she supported her father's Bull Moose Party rather than Longworth's Republicans, and she opposed her distant cousin, Democrat Franklin Roosevelt, when he ran for president in 1932—though she did vote for Democrat Lyndon Johnson in 1964. By her death at age ninety-six she had become a national institution, singlehandedly raising acerbity to an art form and embodying the maxim that women should be both seen and heard as often, as unfettered, and as scathingly frank and funny as possible.

Prints and Photographs Division
LC-J601-100025

s	m	t	w	t	f	s
	1	2	3	4	5	6
7	8	9	10	11	12	13
14	15	16	17	18	19	20
21	22	23	24	25	26	27
28	29	30	31			

july

Artist Käthe Kollwitz b. 1867 — *monday* **8** 189

Poet June Jordan b. 1936 — *tuesday* **9** 190

First meeting of the National Women's Political Caucus is held, 1971 — *wednesday* **10** 191

Susan Warner, author of *The Wide, Wide World,* the first novel to sell one million copies in the U.S., b. 1819 — *thursday* **11** 192

BANK HOLIDAY (N. IRELAND)
Norwegian soprano Kirsten Flagstad b. 1895 — *friday* **12** 193

Pilot Cora Sterling becomes the first female aerial police officer in Seattle, Wash., 1934 — *saturday* **13** 194

Author, mountaineer, and archaeologist Gertrude Bell b. 1868 — *sunday* **14** 195

July

DOROTHY MAYNOR
American (1910–1996)
Concert singer, arts educator

Denied the opera stage because she was African American, Dorothy Maynor nonetheless persevered in a lifetime of glorious singing. Her lyrical, pure soprano graced concert halls throughout the United States, Europe, and Australia. While she was a student at Hampton Institute, noted choirmaster R. Nathaniel Dett encouraged Maynor to pursue a musical career. In 1939 Serge Koussevitsky, calling her voice "a miracle," hired her to perform with the Boston Symphony. Praised for her rendition of lieder, spirituals, and works by Mozart, Handel, and Bach—as well as dozens of operatic arias, especially "Depuis le jour" from Gustave Charpentier's *Louise*—Maynor was also a popular broadcast and recording artist. Shortly after her retirement from singing in 1963, she began giving piano lessons to twelve children in a church annex in Harlem. This soon grew into the Harlem School of the Arts, which she directed until 1979. In 1975 Maynor, who had not been allowed to sing at the Metropolitan Opera during her operatic career, became the first African American on its board of directors.

Prints and Photographs Division
LC-USZ62-102512

s	m	t	w	t	f	s
	1	2	3	4	5	6
7	8	9	10	11	12	13
14	15	16	17	18	19	20
21	22	23	24	25	26	27
28	29	30	31			

july

Novelist Iris Murdoch (*A Severed Head*) b. 1919

monday
15 196

Journalist and antilynching crusader Ida Wells-Barnet b. 1862

tuesday
16 197

Australian novelist Christina Stead b. 1902

wednesday
☽ **17** 198

Geraldine A. Ferraro is nominated for vice president of the U.S., 1984

thursday
18 199

"We hold these truths to be self-evident: that all men and women are created equal. . . ." Declaration of Sentiments is adopted at the first U.S. women's rights convention, Seneca Falls, N.Y., 1848

friday
19 200

U.S. Senator Barbara Mikulski b. 1936

saturday
20 201

Louise Bethune, first female American architect, b. 1856

sunday
21 202

PERLE MESTA

American (1889–1975)
Socialite, diplomat, women's rights
advocate

When Perle Mesta's husband died,
she decided to take his place on the
board of directors of his machine
manufacturing plant. As the other
directors tried to talk her out of it,
she "began to realize that these
eight board members were, after all,
only men," and she stuck to her
decision. The spirited, personable
Mesta, known as "the hostess with
the mostest" for her formidable
entertaining skills, charmed presidents and foreign dignitaries alike.
Her celebrated dinner parties were
almost an adjunct of good government—"Socializing brings people
together and getting people together
promotes better understanding of
common problems," she wrote in
her 1960 autobiography. An effective lobbyist and fundraiser, Mesta
served on the finance committee
of the 1948 Democratic presidential
campaign. As a member of the
National Women's Party, she
ardently supported passage of the
Equal Rights for Women amendment to the Constitution. From
1949 to 1953, Mesta was the first
U.S. ambassador to Luxembourg, a
role that inspired the 1950 Irving
Berlin musical *Call Me Madam.*

s	m	t	w	t	f	s
	1	2	3	4	5	6
7	8	9	10	11	12	13
14	15	16	17	18	19	20
21	22	23	24	25	26	27
28	29	30	31			

july

Author and etiquette authority Amy Vanderbilt b. 1908

monday
22
203

Harriet Strong, agriculturist who patented water storage dams, b. 1844

tuesday
23
204

Wildlife biologist and elephant researcher Cynthia Moss b. 1940

wednesday
24
205

Annette Abbott Adams is sworn in as the first female district attorney of the United States (Northern California District), 1918

thursday
25
206

Burmese human rights leader Aung San Suu Kyi is placed under house arrest, 1989

friday
26
207

Skater and Olympic gold medalist Dorothy Hamill b. 1956

saturday
27
208

Elizabeth Ellery Bailey is confirmed as the first female member of the Civil Aeronautics Board, 1977

sunday
28
209

Mine, gratefully,

Myrtilla Miner

Myrtilla Miner

American (1815–1864)
Educator

"Let us leave 'footprints' that cannot be mistaken," wrote Myrtilla Miner, who believed her commitment to educate African American women was a response to "that high sense of the world's call to everyone who dares to move one step further and enlarge the arena of freedom so much to every soul who shall come after and ask room to move." Miner cherished her own independence, becoming a teacher to support herself. A New York native, in 1847 she taught at a female academy in Mississippi where she was horrified by slavery. After her request to teach African American girls was refused, she returned north, opening the Colored Girls School in Washington, D.C., in 1851. Miner focused on teacher training, and by 1858, six of her pupils were teaching in their own schools. Although threats forced the school to move three times in two years, she was even willing to brandish a pistol to defend her project, and only ill health forced her to stop teaching.

s	m	t	w	t	f	s
				1	2	3
4	5	6	7	8	9	10
11	12	13	14	15	16	17
18	19	20	21	22	23	24
25	26	27	28	29	30	31

august

Volleyball legend Flo Hyman b. 1954

monday
29 210

Emma Gillett, cofounder of Washington College of Law, b. 1852

tuesday
30 211

Russian theosophist and traveler Helena Blavatsky b. 1831

wednesday
31 212

Harriet Quimby becomes the first licensed female pilot in the U.S., 1911

thursday
1 213

Actor Myrna Loy b. 1905

friday
2 214

Mystery novelist P. D. (Phyllis Dorothy) James b. 1920

saturday
3 215

Susanna Wright, Pennsylvania frontierswoman who served as scribe, arbiter, and physician to the Conestoga Indians, b. 1697

sunday
4 216

TAMAKI MIURA

Japanese (1884–1946)
Opera singer

Praised by renowned composer
Giacomo Puccini as the ideal
Madame Butterfly, Tamaki Miura
breached the conventions for
women in her country to become
an international opera star. Miura
persuaded her father to allow her to
study music by agreeing to marry.
Upon completing her program, she
divorced her first husband, remar-
rying later for love. She made her
opera debut in Tokyo, but sang for
most of her career in England, the
United States, and Italy. In 1915
she gave a stunning performance
as Butterfly in Boston and repeated
the role many times, singing in
England under the direction of
the eminent conductor Sir Thomas
Beecham. Miura premiered Aldo
Franchetti's *Namiko-San* at the
Chicago Civic Opera, a role created
especially for her, and gave the
first American performance of
Andre-Charles-Prosper Messager's
Madame Chrysantheme. All three
roles became staples of her reper-
toire, but she also sang classical
Western parts. In 1932 Miura
retired to the Japanese country-
side, where she continued singing
for the enjoyment of the local
population.

Photograph by Arnold Genthe
Prints and Photographs Division
LC-G432–1155

s	m	t	w	t	f	s
				1	2	3
4	5	6	7	8	9	10
11	12	13	14	15	16	17
18	19	20	21	22	23	24
25	26	27	28	29	30	31

august

BANK HOLIDAY (SCOTLAND)
Historian Mary Ritter Beard (*Woman as a Force in History*)
b. 1876

monday
5   217

Queen Wilhelmina of the Netherlands becomes the first reign-
ing queen to address a joint session of U.S. Congress, 1941

tuesday
6   218

Mata Hari b. 1876

wednesday
7   219

Marjorie Kinnan Rawlings, winner of the 1939 Pulitzer Prize
for *The Yearling,* b. 1896

thursday
●**8**   220

Singer Whitney Houston b. 1963

friday
9   221

Anna J. Cooper, black educator and president of Frelinghuysen
University, b. 1859

saturday
10   222

Sarah Bernhardt makes her stage debut in *Iphigenie,* Paris, 1862

sunday
11   223

MARIANNE CRAIG MOORE
American (1887–1972)
Poet

"Poetry," said Marianne Moore, "watches life with affection." A mosaicist with words, Moore created her own disciplined verse from countless small observations: elephants pushing; imperial floor coverings of coach-wheel yellow; the moves of a baseball player; the flamingo-colored, maple leaf–like feet of a swan under the willows in Oxford. Born in St. Louis, educated at Bryn Mawr, and sometime teacher and librarian, Moore entered the world of poetry by first contributing to the English magazine *The Egoist*. Volumes of poetry followed, which gained her awards and honors. Regardless of her fame as a poet, Moore once stated that her work was categorized as poetry only because it didn't fit anyplace else. And in the poem "Poetry," she offered a further revelation:

"I, too, dislike it: there are things that are important beyond all this fiddle. / Reading it, however, with a perfect contempt for it, one discovers in / it after all, a place for the genuine."

Prints and Photographs Division
LC-U5Z62-101955

s	m	t	w	t	f	s
				1	2	3
4	5	6	7	8	9	10
11	12	13	14	15	16	17
18	19	20	21	22	23	24
25	26	27	28	29	30	31

august

Katharine Lee Bates, poet and author of "America the Beautiful," b. 1859

monday **12** 224

Abolitionist and suffragist Lucy Stone b. 1818

tuesday **13** 225

Jockey Robyn Smith b. 1944

wednesday **14** 226

Author and broadcaster Linda Ellerbee b. 1944

thursday ☽ **15** 227

Author Margaret Mitchell, age 48, dies after being hit by a drunk driver, 1949

friday **16** 228

Laura de Force Gordon, newspaperwoman and pioneer California suffragist, b. 1838

saturday **17** 229

Tennessee becomes the 36th and final state to ratify the 19th Amendment (woman suffrage), 1920

sunday **18** 230

SUSHILA NAYAR

Indian (1914–2001)
Physician, political activist

By the time India achieved its freedom from British rule in 1949, Sushila Nayar was already a close political ally of Mahatma Mohandas Gandhi. She had served as his personal physician, and had spent two years in prison with other leaders of the independence movement—an extraordinary life's achievement in itself, but only a prelude to a fifty-year career in medicine and public service. While Nayar cared for the Mahatma, she also established a dispensary for the villagers who lived near him. She went on to serve as the Health Minister of Delhi State, where she introduced programs to combat malaria, tuberculosis, and leprosy, established emergency services in New Delhi, and in 1969 founded and began to teach at the Mahatma Gandhi Institute of Medical Sciences. Nayar's influence in developing medical programs and training in India was matched by the respect she earned for her dedication to the Gandhian philosophy of nonviolent protest. She wrote several volumes on his life and work.

s	m	t	w	t	f	s
				1	2	3
4	5	6	7	8	9	10
11	12	13	14	15	16	17
18	19	20	21	22	23	24
25	26	27	28	29	30	31

august

Prison reformer Mary Belle Harris b. 1874

monday
19 231

The Abbey Theatre is founded in Dublin by Lady Gregory and William Butler Yeats, 1904

tuesday
20 232

Composer Lili Boulanger b. 1893

wednesday
21 233

Katherine Anne Porter embarks on the voyage—from Veracruz, Mexico, to Bremerhaven, Germany—that will serve as the setting for her 1962 novel *Ship of Fools*, 1931.

thursday
22 234

Sarah Whiting, physicist and astronomer, b. 1847

friday
23 235

Nature writer and mystic Margaret Fairless Barber ("Michael Fairless") dies in England at age 32 after a long illness, 1901

saturday
24 236

Malvina Reynolds, singer, composer, and activist, b. 1900

sunday
25 237

MAUD WOOD PARK

American (1871–1955)
Suffragist

Maud Wood Park was an American suffragist whose lobbying skills and political savvy made her a key figure in the early feminist movement. A brilliant student at Radcliffe College in the 1890s, Park was shocked to find herself surrounded by antisuffragists and again dismayed to be one of the youngest representatives at the 1900 convention of the National American Woman Suffrage Association in Washington, D.C. This prompted her to organize the College of Equal Suffrage League, which rallied widespread support among women of her generation. In 1916, Park, a Bostonian, moved to Washington to head the congressional committee of the National American Woman Suffrage Association. Her understanding of the legislative process contributed immeasurably to the passage of the Nineteenth Amendment granting women the right to vote. When the National League of Women Voters was established in 1920, Park was chosen to be its first president. She also organized the Women's Joint Congressional Committee, which effectively sought federal aid for women's and children's health and welfare programs.

Prints and Photographs Division
  LC-USZ62-93551

s	m	t	w	t	f	s
1	2	3	4	5	6	7
8	9	10	11	12	13	14
15	16	17	18	19	20	21
22	23	24	25	26	27	28
29	30					

september

BANK HOLIDAY (U.K. EXCEPT SCOTLAND)
The 19th Amendment formally takes effect: "The right of citizens of the United States to vote shall not be denied or abridged . . . on account of sex," 1920

monday
26 238

Sophia Smith, founder of Smith College, b. 1910

tuesday
27 239

Rita Dove, author, educator, and Poet Laureate of the U.S., b. 1952

wednesday
28 240

Singer Dinah Washington b. 1924

thursday
29 241

Frankenstein author Mary Wollstonecraft Shelley b. 1797

friday
30 242

Educator Maria Montessori b. 1870

saturday
☾ **31** 243

Naturalist Anna Botsford Comstock b. 1854

sunday
1 244

September

SARA PAYSON WILLIS PARTON

American (1811–1872)
Journalist, author

In 1853, Sara Willis Parton accomplished something nearly unheard of for a woman: she published a collection of columns, *Fern Leaves from Fanny's Port-Folio*, which sold almost 100,000 copies within a year, enabling her to buy a home for herself and her children. Parton began writing short magazine pieces under the name Fanny Fern after her first husband died and her second husband left her. Her autobiographical novel *Ruth Hall* (1855)—in which a widow becomes independent and successful through her own efforts, despite poor treatment by her relatives—was praised by suffragist Elizabeth Cady Stanton and novelist Nathaniel Hawthorne, but attacked by most male critics for its unladylike lack of delicacy. For twenty years, Parton wrote a weekly column for the *New York Ledger*, making her one of the first American newspaper columnists of her gender. At first sentimental, her work grew to embrace satirical commentary on domestic life, moving descriptions of social ills, and support for the vote and expanding opportunities for women.

Prints and Photographs Division
LC-USZ62-90648

s	m	t	w	t	f	s
1	2	3	4	5	6	7
8	9	10	11	12	13	14
5	16	17	18	19	20	21
2	23	24	25	26	27	28
9	30					

september

LABOR DAY (U.S., CANADA)
Christa McAuliffe, first teacher in space, b. 1948

monday
2   245

Texas politician and governor Ann Richards b. 1933

tuesday
3   246

Katherine Biddle, popular U.S. poet of the 1920s, b. 1902

wednesday
4   247

Pianist and composer Amy Beach b. 1867

thursday
5   248

ROSH HASHANAH (BEGINS AT SUNSET)
Jane Addams b. 1860

friday
6   249

Marge Simpson (Julie Kavner) b. 1951

saturday
7   250

Hani Mokoto, Japanese journalist and educator, b. 1873

sunday
8   251

September

ANNIE SMITH PECK
American (1850–1935)
Mountaineer, scholar

It was Annie Smith Peck, the first U.S. woman climber to achieve renown, who planted the "Votes for Women" pennant atop Peru's Mount Coropuna in 1911. The daughter of a Rhode Island coal merchant, Peck put herself through the University of Michigan, taught Latin at Purdue University (1881–1883), and was pursuing further study in music, languages, and classical archaeology when an 1885 trip to Switzerland gave her her first taste of mountain climbing. Immediately hooked, she taught in the U.S. to raise money for her new passion. Peck's first major ascent, of California's Mount Shasta (1891), was followed four years later by a climb up the Matterhorn (in dress like that shown here; the lack of skirts drew as much attention as her feat.) After scaling all the major peaks of Europe, she turned to South America, a continent that interested her for its peoples and cultures as well as its topography. Her 1908 ascent of Peru's highest peak, Mount Huscaran—after two unsuccessful attempts—brought her worldwide fame.

Prints and Photographs Division
LC-USZ62-118273

s	m	t	w	t	f	s
1	2	3	4	5	6	7
8	9	10	11	12	13	14
15	16	17	18	19	20	21
22	23	24	25	26	27	28
29	30					

september

Author Phyllis Whitney b. 1903

monday
9 252

Women's Auxiliary Ferrying Squadron (WAFS) established, 1942

tuesday
10 253

Rosika Schwimmer, pacifist and internationalist, b. 1877

wednesday
11 254

Actor Margaret Hamilton, dean of cinematic wicked witches, b. 1902

thursday
12 255

Author Judith Martin (a.k.a. Miss Manners) b. 1938

friday
☽**13** 256

Birth control advocate Margaret Sanger b. 1879

saturday
14 257

YOM KIPPUR (BEGINS AT SUNSET)
Louise B. Bethune becomes first woman architect elected to AIA, 1890

sunday
15 258

September

MAUD POWELL
American (1868–1920)
Violinist

A child prodigy who made her first musical tour at age nine, Maud Powell was the first American violinist—man or woman—to achieve international stature. At thirteen she left her home in Illinois to study in Europe; soon thereafter, she performed for Queen Victoria. She made her orchestral debut with the Berlin Philharmonic in 1885, and in the same year played with the New York Philharmonic, establishing herself as a star on both sides of the Atlantic. Known for her technical mastery as well as a gift for interpretation, Powell often performed contemporary music, premiering fourteen violin concertos before American audiences. She was just as popular with the musically sophisticated audiences of Europe. Her success made her the obvious choice to inaugurate the Victor Talking Machine Company's Celebrity Artist Series on the Red Seal label. Throughout her life, Powell voiced her belief that women were as capable as men in both performance and composition, something she superbly confirmed every time she appeared on stage.

Prints and Photographs Division
LC-USZ62–110623

s	m	t	w	t	f	s
1	2	3	4	5	6	7
8	9	10	11	12	13	14
15	16	17	18	19	20	21
22	23	24	25	26	27	28
29	30					

september

Ella Crandall, pioneer of visiting-nurse programs, b. 1871

monday
16   259

Maureen Connolly, first woman to win the "grand slam" in tennis, b. 1934

tuesday
17   260

Religious rebel Anne Hutchinson arrives in Boston from England, 1634

wednesday
18   261

Pop singer "Mama" Cass Elliott b. 1941

thursday
19   262

Billie Jean King beats Bobby Riggs in the "Battle of the Sexes" tennis match, Houston, 1973

friday
20   263

Playwright Marsha Norman b. 1947

saturday
21   264

Judge Sandra Day O'Connor's nomination to the U.S. Supreme Court is confirmed, 1981

sunday
22   265

September

MARY QUANT

English (b. 1934)
Fashion designer, businesswoman

The only person to be awarded the [British] *Sunday Times* International Award for "Jolting England out of its Conventional Attitude towards clothes," Mary Quant blazed new trails in the fashion world of the 1960s with her youth-oriented designs. "I think that I broke the couture stranglehold that Chanel, Dior and the others had on fashion, when I created styles at the working-girl level," she speculated. "It all added up to a democratization of fashion and entertainment." Quant was the leading figure in the "mod" revolution, creating clothes with bold colors and patterns, as well as "an innocent, child look" of simple, skinny lines and short skirts. She did more than any other designer to popularize the miniskirt, and added hot pants to her credits in 1969. Without any business experience, Quant went from successful shop owner to manufacturer for an international market. In 1966 she received the Order of the British Empire for her contribution to fashion, wearing her signature miniskirt and cutaway gloves.

s	m	t	w	t	f	s
1	2	3	4	5	6	7
8	9	10	11	12	13	14
15	16	17	18	19	20	21
22	23	24	25	26	27	28
29	30					

september

AUTUMNAL EQUINOX 4:56 A.M. (GMT)
Antinuclear activist Mary Sinclair b. 1918

monday
23 · 266

Poet and activist Frances E. W. Harper b. 1825

tuesday
24 · 267

Broadcast journalist Barbara Walters b. 1931

wednesday
25 · 268

Country music star Lynn Anderson b. 1947

thursday
26 · 269

Sarah De Crow, first woman postmaster, b. 1792

friday
27 · 270

Blues singer Koko Taylor b. 1935

saturday
28 · 271

Congress passes Equal Credit Opportunity Act, 1974

sunday
29 · 272

GEORGE SAND

French (1804–1876)
Author

Although George Sand dared nineteenth-century society in many ways—she wore men's clothing, smoked a pipe, wrote passionate novels, had numerous love affairs with celebrated artists such as Frédéric Chopin, wrote political tracts promoting the 1848 uprising that established the Second French Republic—she was perhaps most daring in the simple fact that she chose to live an independent life, a model of women's equality with men. Born Aurore Dupin and raised largely by her aristocratic grandmother, she married a baron at age eighteen. In 1831 she left that supremely unhappy marriage for the freedom of Paris. As she wrote in 1837, "We cannot tear out a single page of our life, but we can throw the whole book in the fire." Her enormously popular first novel, *Indiana*, portrayed marriage as a kind of slavery for women. Sand published prolifically to support her two children, including fiction exploring Christian socialism and pastoral life, plays, essays, and an autobiography that still inspires women to live out their ideals.

s	m	t	w	t	f	s
		1	2	3	4	5
6	7	8	9	10	11	12
13	14	15	16	17	18	19
20	21	22	23	24	25	26
27	28	29	30	31		

october

Sally Ride blasts off on six-day *Challenger* flight, 1983

monday
30 273

Entertainer Julie Andrews b. 1935

tuesday
1 274

Designer Donna Karan b. 1948

wednesday
2 275

Rebecca Felton becomes the first woman to occupy a seat in the U.S. Senate, 1922

thursday
3 276

Bernice Johnson Reagon, historian, musician, and activist, b. 1942

friday
4 277

Architect Maya Ying Lin, designer of the Vietnam Veterans Memorial, b. 1959

saturday
5 278

Fannie Lou Hamer, sharecropper and voting rights activist, b. 1917

sunday
6 279

DIANA SANDS

American (1934–1973)
Actress

"The Negro female has been characterized as the neuter, a mammy, an exotic. Why isn't she a mother, wife . . . a woman desired . . . someone who embodies all the characteristics of American womanhood?" once asked African American actress Diane Sands, whose refusal to play stereotypical roles was a hallmark of her theatrical career. In 1964, the same year that Congress passed the Civil Rights Act ending segregation, Sands starred on Broadway in *The Owl and the Pussycat*, playing a role written for a white woman, to rave reviews. She later appeared in film and television, but also pursued her long-standing interest in performing the classic stage roles written for women. Again, she met opposition because of racial stereotypes, but nonetheless starred in *Caesar and Cleopatra*, *Antony and Cleopatra*, and *Phaedra*, and as George Bernard Shaw's *St. Joan*, considered by critics the pinnacle of a brilliant career. Sands was a founder of Third World Cinema, a company which brought her freedom from discrimination and greater control of her work.

Prints and Photographs Division
LC-USZ62-103688

s	m	t	w	t	f	s
		1	2	3	4	5
6	7	8	9	10	11	12
13	14	15	16	17	18	19
20	21	22	23	24	25	26
27	28	29	30	31		

october

Toni Morrison is awarded the Nobel Prize in literature, 1993

monday
7 280

Actor Sigourney Weaver b. 1949

tuesday
8 281

Actor Helen Hayes b. 1900

wednesday
9 282

Beatrice Hinkle, first female public health physician, b. 1874

thursday
10 283

Marguerite d'Angouleme, queen consort of Henry II of Navarre, patron of humanists and religious reformers, and author, b. 1492

friday
11 284

COLUMBUS DAY
Red Cross leader Mabel Boardman b. 1860

saturday
12 285

Pioneering African American jurist Edith Spurlock Sampson b. 1901

sunday
☽ **13** 286

October

DOROTHY SAYERS

English (1893–1957)
Writer, scholar

With the publication of *Whose Body?* in 1923, British writer Dorothy L. Sayers introduced Lord Peter Wimsey to the public. The witty, aristocratic detective appeared in her subsequent best-selling crime novels, including *The Nine Tailors* and *Gaudy Night.* Erudite and complexly plotted, the books continue to be the most read and admired texts in their genre. The only child of the Reverend Henry Sayers, Dorothy was born in Oxford on June 13, 1893. One of the first women to receive a degree from the University of Oxford, she graduated with honors in modern languages. In addition to crime fiction, Sayers published theological studies, plays, and accomplished literary translations: notably Dante's *Divine Comedy* from Italian and *Song of Roland* from Old French. A formidable woman who used her pen to fight intellectual battles, Sayers encountered opposition to some of her religious works, but was undaunted by challenges to her philosophy. Uncompromising in her art, she died of heart failure in 1957.

New York World-Telegram & Sun
  Collection
  Prints and Photographs Division
  LC-USZ62–112724

s	m	t	w	t	f	s
		1	2	3	4	5
6	7	8	9	10	11	12
13	14	15	16	17	18	19
20	21	22	23	24	25	26
27	28	29	30	31		

october

COLUMBUS DAY OBSERVED
THANKSGIVING DAY (CANADA)
Author Katherine Mansfield b. 1888

monday
14   287

Author and Indian rights agitator Helen Hunt Jackson b. 1830

tuesday
15   288

Margaret Sanger opens the first U.S. birth control clinic, New York City, 1916

wednesday
16   289

Physician and astronaut Mae C. Jemison b. 1956

thursday
17   290

Martina Navratilova, tennis great and gay-rights spokeswoman, b. 1956

friday
18   291

Mountaineer Annie Smith Peck b. 1850

saturday
19   292

Byllye Avery, founder of the Black Women's Health Network, b. 1937

sunday
20   293

October

MURIEL SIEBERT

American (b. 1932)
Financier

One of Muriel Siebert's favorite words is "risk." As the first woman to own a seat on the New York Stock Exchange and the first to head one of its member firms, she has unabashedly advised that "the men of the top of industry and government should be more willing to risk sharing leadership with women and minority members . . . we need the different viewpoints and experiences, we need the enlarged talent bank." A Cleveland native, Siebert never graduated from college, but managed to work her way up to a partnership in a leading Wall Street brokerage firm. Still, when she applied to become a member of the New York Stock Exchange in 1967, nine of the ten men she asked to sponsor her application turned her down. She was finally elected to membership on December 28, 1967. In 1977, she was appointed superintendent of New York State's Banking Department. The acknowledged "first woman of finance" now heads the successful firm of Muriel Siebert & Co.

New York World-Telegram & Sun
Collection
Prints and Photographs Division
LC-USZ62–125103

s	m	t	w	t	f	s
		1	2	3	4	5
6	7	8	9	10	11	12
13	14	15	16	17	18	19
20	21	22	23	24	25	26
27	28	29	30	31		

october

Grete Waitz becomes the first woman to run a marathon in under 2.5 hours, New York City, 1979

monday
21 294

Abigail Scott Duniway, Oregon journalist and lecturer on women's rights, b. 1834

tuesday
22 295

Long-distance swimmer Gertrude Ederle b. 1906

wednesday
23 296

UNITED NATIONS DAY
Pioneering lawyer and U.S. presidential candidate Belva Lockwood b. 1830

thursday
24 297

Hanna Holborn Gray, president of the University of Chicago, b. 1930

friday
25 298

Hillary Rodham Clinton, the first First Lady to be elected to the U.S. Senate, b. 1947

saturday
26 299

DAYLIGHT SAVING TIME ENDS
SUMMER TIME ENDS (U.K.)
Author Maxine Hong Kingston b. 1940

sunday
27 300

AILEEN RIGGIN SOULE

American (b. 1906)
Athlete

Few champions have begun so early and continued so long as Aileen Riggin Soule, the youngest Olympic gold medalist when she clinched the springboard diving competition in 1920 at age fourteen. Since there were no swimming pools deep enough for the Brooklyn native to dive in—the one at the New York Athletic Club didn't admit women— she practiced diving in a tidal pool at the beach. At the 1924 Olympic Games, Soule became the first athlete, and the only American, to compete in both swimming and diving events, garnering a bronze and a silver medal. After turning pro in 1926, she gave diving exhibitions throughout the world and appeared in several Hollywood films. She was also one of the first women sportswriters, contributing to national magazines. Soule has never stopped swimming. She set freestyle and backstroke world records in her eighties, and at age ninety—still going strong—enjoyed thirteen first-place finishes and set eleven national and five world records for the 90–94 age group.

Prints and Photographs Division
LC-USZ62-113425

s	m	t	w	t	f	s
					1	2
3	4	5	6	7	8	9
0	11	12	13	14	15	16
7	18	19	20	21	22	23
4	25	26	27	28	29	30

november

Suffragist and orator Anna Dickinson b. 1842

monday
28 301

National Organization for Women (NOW) is founded, 1966

tuesday
☾ **29** 302

Gertrude Atherton, who pioneered the biographical novel form with *The Conqueror* (1902), b. 1857

wednesday
30 303

HALLOWEEN
Singer and actor Ethel Waters b. 1900

thursday
31 304

Boston Female Medical School established, 1848

friday
1 305

Singer k. d. lang b. 1961

saturday
2 306

Comedian and television mogul Roseanne b. 1952

sunday
3 307

November

HELEN STEPHENS
American (1918–1994)
Athlete

Helen Stephens—the "Fulton Flash" from a farm in Fulton, Missouri— dazzled the sports world with her sprinting ability (she never lost a sprint), but the versatile athlete also competed in weight events and played pro basketball and softball. When she took the gold in the 1936 Olympic 100-meter dash in 11.5 seconds, Stephens set a world record that went unbroken for twenty-four years. She also won a gold medal as a member of the 100-meter relay team, and placed ninth in the discus throw, later earning three more national titles in track and shot put before she turned pro in 1937. The next year, Stephens established the Helen Stephens Olympic Co-Eds, becoming the first woman to own and manage a semiprofessional women's basketball team. The group played until 1952, although Stephens took time out to serve in the U.S. Marine Corps during World War II. In the 1980s she again competed in masters track and field events, maintaining her undefeated record.

New York World-Telegram & Sun
Collection
Prints and Photographs Division
LC-USZ62–116387

s	m	t	w	t	f	s
					1	2
3	4	5	6	7	8	9
10	11	12	13	14	15	16
17	18	19	20	21	22	23
24	25	26	27	28	29	30

november

Carol Moseley-Braun becomes the first African American woman elected to the U.S. Senate, 1992
monday
4 308

ELECTION DAY
Pioneering investigative journalist Ida Tarbell b. 1857
tuesday
5 309

Tania Aebi completes a solo 27-month sailing voyage around the world, 1987
wednesday
6 310

Singer and songwriter Joni Mitchell b. 1943
thursday
7 311

Bonnie Raitt, first woman to have a signature model Fender Stratocaster electric guitar, b. 1949
friday
8 312

Poet Anne Sexton b. 1928
saturday
9 313

English Anglican church votes to ordain women as priests, 1993
sunday
10 314

November

JUANITA KIDD STOUT
American (1919–1998)
Judge

Juanita Kidd Stout's life reflects the momentous changes brought about by the civil rights movement in the mid-twentieth century. As a child in Oklahoma, she attended segregated schools, yet she went on to become the first African American woman to both be elected as a judge to a court of record and serve on a state supreme court. Stout earned a B.A. in music attending the University of Iowa because she did not want to study at Oklahoma's college for black students, which was unaccredited. She received two law degrees from Indiana University. After a stint as an assistant district attorney in Philadelphia—the D.A. called her "the hardest-working lawyer in town"—she was elected to the Philadelphia court of common pleas in 1959, and resoundingly reelected twice. In 1988 she began her tenure on the Pennsylvania Supreme Court, and later served again on the court of common pleas. Throughout her career she was praised for her compassion and unswerving sense of justice.

New York World-Telegram & Sun
    Collection
    Prints and Photographs Division
    LC-USZ62-122228

s	m	t	w	t	f	s
					1	2
	4	5	6	7	8	9
	11	12	13	14	15	16
	18	19	20	21	22	23
	25	26	27	28	29	30

november

VETERANS' DAY
REMEMBRANCE DAY (CANADA)
Abigail Adams b. 1744

monday
☽ 11 315

Suffrage leader and freethinker Elizabeth Cady Stanton b. 1815

tuesday
12 316

Comedian and actor Whoopi Goldberg b. 1955

wednesday
13 317

Claribel Cone, benefactor of the Baltimore Museum of Art, b. 1864

thursday
14 318

Painter Georgia O'Keeffe b. 1887

friday
15 319

Paula Giddings, author and historian of African American women, b. 1947

saturday
16 320

Religious leader Anne Hutchinson, convicted of "traducing the ministers," is banished from the Massachusetts Bay Colony, 1637

sunday
17 321

KAY SWIFT

American (1897–1993)
Composer, lyricist

In 1930, when Tin Pan Alley was a man's world, Kay Swift opened on Broadway with *Fine and Dandy*, the first Broadway musical whose score was written entirely by a woman. Her hit show ran for 236 performances, and the title song became a standard still sung today. Swift began her career as a classical musician: she attended the Institute of Musical Arts (now Juilliard) and the New England Conservatory, where she studied counterpoint and orchestration, and toured as an accompanist on the piano. Then she met George Gershwin, who transformed her perception of popular music. Swift wrote her first hit song, "Can't We Be Friends?" in 1929, and added scores for Radio City Music Hall and for a 1950 movie based on her life, *Never a Dull Moment*, to her credit. She was still composing in her nineties. Swift worked with Gershwin on many pieces, including *Porgy and Bess*, and made a significant contribution to American music by cataloging his unpublished compositions after his death.

New York World-Telegram & Sun Collection
Prints and Photographs Division
LC-USZ62-121177

s	m	t	w	t	f	s
					1	2
3	4	5	6	7	8	9
0	11	12	13	14	15	16
7	18	19	20	21	22	23
4	25	26	27	28	29	30

november

Cherokee nation leader Wilma Mankiller b. 1945

monday
18 322

Indian stateswoman Indira Gandhi b. 1917

tuesday
19 323

Pauli Murray, lawyer, civil rights activist, and priest, b. 1910

wednesday
20 324

Actor and feminist Marlo Thomas b. 1938

thursday
21 325

Billie Jean King, tennis great and women's sports advocate, b. 1943

friday
22 326

Marie Van Vorst, author and reformer who exposed working conditions of women in factories, b. 1867

saturday
23 327

Nautical folk heroine Grace Darling b. 1815

sunday
24 328

Nov/Dec

SOJOURNER TRUTH

American (1797–1883)
Abolitionist, women's rights activist

Feminist in an abolitionist movement dominated by men; activist for African American rights in a suffragist movement dominated by white middle-class women: Sojourner Truth was an electrifying presence in the struggle for equal rights. Born a slave with the name Isabella Baumfree, Truth escaped servitude in 1828 under the New York State Anti-Slavery Act. She changed her name to Sojourner Truth when she responded to "a call from God" and became an itinerant preacher. An imposing six feet tall, Truth was a powerful and eloquent speaker, despite her lack of formal education. She was second to none in her belief in the power of women: "If the first woman God ever made was strong enough to turn the world upside down all alone," she said in her famous "Ain't I a Woman?" speech at the 1851 Women's Convention, "these women together ought to be able to turn it back, and get it right side up again! And now they is asking to do it, the men better let them."

General Collections

s	m	t	w	t	f	s
1	2	3	4	5	6	7
8	9	10	11	12	13	14
15	16	17	18	19	20	21
22	23	24	25	26	27	28
29	30	31				

december

Temperance hellraiser Carry Nation b. 1846
monday
25 329

Abolitionist and suffragist Sarah Grimke b. 1792
tuesday
26 330

Elsie Clews Parsons, pioneering anthropologist and teacher, b. 1875
wednesday
27 331

THANKSGIVING DAY
Helen Magill White, educator and first U.S. woman to earn a Ph.D (1877), b. 1853
thursday
28 332

HANUKKAH (BEGINS AT SUNSET)
Nellie Tayloe Ross, first female U.S. governor (Wyoming, 1925–1927) and director of the Mint, b. 1876
friday
29 333

FIRST DAY OF HANUKKAH
Shirley Chisholm, first black U.S. congresswoman and presidential candidate, b. 1924
saturday
30 334

Ann Preston, physician and founder of the Women's Hospital in Philadelphia, b. 1813
sunday
1 335

December

BERTHA VON SUTTNER
Czech/Austrian (1843–1914)
Peace activist, author

Born Countess Bertha Felicie Sophie Kinsky in Prague, Bertha von Suttner was the first woman to win a Nobel Prize—and the first to win the Nobel Peace Prize. A leader and symbol of the late nineteenth century's international peace movement, she was a prolific writer with a strong pacifist philosophy. In 1889 she published her most famous novel, *Die Waffen nieder (Lay Down Your Arms)*, a thoroughly researched, powerful book exposing the devastation of war. She helped to set up peace societies, attended conferences and congresses, lectured widely, and founded, edited, and wrote for a peace journal. Her letters to Alfred Nobel kept him abreast of pacifist activities, leading him to establish the Nobel Peace Prize. Von Suttner commanded international respect at a time when few women achieved the stature of public leadership. She continued to champion her cause in the new century, and died shortly before the outbreak of World War I—a conflict she had foreseen and warned against, but could not prevent.

s	m	t	w	t	f	s
1	2	3	4	5	6	7
8	9	10	11	12	13	14
5	16	17	18	19	20	21
2	23	24	25	26	27	28
9	30	31				

december

Tennis champ Monica Seles b. 1973

monday
2 336

Opera legend Maria Callas b. 1923

tuesday
3 337

Edith Cavell, nurse and patriot, b. 1865

wednesday
● **4** 338

Elizabeth Agassiz, educator and first president of Radcliffe College, b. 1822

thursday
5 339

Patsy Mink, first Japanese American congresswoman and author of the Women's Educational Equity Act, b. 1927

friday
6 340

Multimedia artist Ellen Stewart b. 1919

saturday
7 341

Singer Sinead O'Connor b. 1966

sunday
8 342

December

LILLIAN WALD

American (1867–1940)
Nurse, public health advocate,
social activist

"Nursing is love in action," observed
Lillian Wald, who left medical school
to meet the desperately immediate
needs of tenement dwellers in New
York. Wald was already a trained
nurse when she began working with
impoverished immigrants on the
Lower East Side. She lived among
them, in 1893 establishing the Henry
Street Settlement, which quickly
evolved into the Visiting Nurse
Society. Wald's program became a
model for public health nursing
services worldwide, but her efforts
did not end there. She began the
first American nursing program for
public schools, convinced Columbia
University to offer the first college-
based education for nurses, persuaded
insurance companies to provide free
nursing to their business policy-
holders, and added social services
to the Henry Street program. Endlessly
energetic and compassionate, Wald
seemed to play an influential role
in every progressive, visionary cause
of her time, from child welfare (Theodore Roosevelt created a Federal
Children's Bureau in response to her
efforts), trade unionism, divorce
law reform, worker safety, and
peace, to woman suffrage.

Photograph by Arnold Genthe
Prints and Photographs Division
LC-G412-9448-006

s	m	t	w	t	f	s
1	2	3	4	5	6	7
8	9	10	11	12	13	14
15	16	17	18	19	20	21
22	23	24	25	26	27	28
29	30	31				

december

Computer language innovator Grace Hopper b. 1906

monday
9 343

Poet Emily Dickinson b. 1830

tuesday
10 344

Astronomer Annie Jump Cannon b. 1863

wednesday
☽ **11** 345

Toshiko Akiyoshi, jazz composer and bandleader, b. 1929

thursday
12 346

Civil rights activist Ella Baker b. 1903

friday
13 347

Senator and congresswoman Margaret Chase Smith b. 1897

saturday
14 348

First women Secret Service agents sworn in, 1971

sunday
15 349

December

MARION POST WOLCOTT

American (1910–1990)
Photographer

A self-taught photographer, New Jersey–born Marion Post (who married Lee Wolcott in 1941) acquired her first camera in Europe in the 1930s. After working as a freelance photographer and for the *Philadelphia Evening Bulletin*, in 1938 she joined the remarkable group of photographers assembled by the U.S. Farm Security Administration to document American life in the years of the Great Depression. On a shoestring budget, she moved through the country, celebrating the endurance of hard-pressed people, documenting the gap between rich and poor—and producing thousands of memorable images, including migrant farm laborers in South Carolina, opulent lifestyles in Miami Beach, and evocative scenes of snow-covered Vermont. After World War II her work became less well known. But in the 1990s a renewed interest in her achievements was reflected in the publication of two books: *Marion Post Wolcott: A Photographic Journey* by F. Jack Hurley and *Looking for the Light: The Hidden Life and Art of Marion Post Wolcott* by Paul Hendrickson.

Prints and Photographs Division
LC-USF34-T01-029245

s	m	t	w	t	f	s
1	2	3	4	5	6	7
8	9	10	11	12	13	14
15	16	17	18	19	20	21
22	23	24	25	26	27	28
29	30	31				

december

Novelist Jane Austen b. 1775

monday
16 350

Deborah Sampson, who, disguised as a man and going by the name Robert Shurtleff, joined the Continental Army and fought in the Revolutionary War, b. 1760

tuesday
17 351

Gladys Henry Dick, microbiologist who isolated the bacterial cause of scarlet fever, b. 1881

wednesday
18 352

Actor Cicely Tyson b. 1933

thursday
○ **19** 353

Ethel Barrymore Theater opens in New York City, 1928

Soccer 8⁴⁰

friday
20 354

Rebecca West, author, critic, and feminist, b. 1892

Solstice Dawn + Sundown

saturday
21 355

WINTER SOLSTICE 1:15 A.M. (GMT)
Theatrical designer Aline Bernstein b. 1880

Soccer 11³⁰ AM

sunday
22 356

December

JANE C. WRIGHT

American (b. 1919)
Physician, researcher

In 1967, Jane C. Wright made history when she attained the highest position held by an African American woman in medical administration in the U.S., associate dean of her alma mater, New York Medical College. Wright, who came from a distinguished family of doctors—her father was one of the first African Americans to graduate from Harvard Medical School, and her grandfather was in one of the first classes at Meharry Medical College—had already distinguished herself for her cancer research. She was a pioneer in testing chemotherapy drugs to record effective dosing levels in humans, and went on to succeed her father as Director of Cancer Research at Harlem Hospital. In 1955 she joined New York University as an associate professor of research surgery. At New York Medical College she not only served as dean and professor of surgery, but directed the college cancer research laboratory until she retired in 1987. Wright's honors include the American Medical Association's Distinguished Service Award in 1965.

Photograph by Irwin Gooen
New York World-Telegram & Sun
Collection
Prints and Photographs Division
LC-USZ62-122231

s	m	t	w	t	f	s
	1	2	3	4	5	6	7
8	9	10	11	12	13	14
15	16	17	18	19	20	21
22	23	24	25	26	27	28
29	30	31				

december

Mme C. J. Walker (Sarah Breedlove), self-made cosmetics magnate and philanthropist, b. 1867

monday
23 357

Ross B+B a.m

Elizabeth Chandler, abolitionist author who supported boycotting goods made by slave labor, b. 1807

tuesday
24 358

CHRISTMAS DAY
Singer Annie Lennox b. 1954

wednesday
25 359

KWANZAA BEGINS
BOXING DAY (CANADA, U.K.)
Sled-dog racing champ Susan Butcher b. 1954

thursday
26 360

Actor and singer Marlene Dietrich b. 1901

friday
27 361

My Day

Oscar-winning actress Maggie Smith b. 1934

saturday
28 362

XMas @ Sheree's

Composer and critic Peggy Glanville-Hicks b. 1912

sunday
29 363

Dec/Jan

ROSALYN YALOW

American (b. 1921)
Physicist

"Perhaps the earliest memories I have are of being a stubborn, determined child," recalled Rosalyn Yalow in 1977, the year she became the first American woman (and the second woman ever) to be awarded the Nobel Prize in Physiology or Medicine. A determined adult as well, she defied discrimination against women in science to earn a doctorate in physics from the University of Illinois. As a physicist at the Veterans Administration Hospital in the Bronx, New York, she collaborated with Dr. Solomon Berson on the application of radioisotopes to medicine. She received her Nobel Prize for developing a method called radioimmunoassay (RIA) that used radioisotopes to detect minute concentrations of substances such as hormones, enzymes, and drugs in blood or other fluids. Yalow, whose work revolutionized biological and medical research, has urged other women to pursue the sciences: "We must believe in ourselves or no one else will believe in us. . . . The world cannot afford the loss of the talents of half its people."

New York World-Telegram & Sun
      Collection
      Prints and Photographs Division
      LC-USZ62–122235

s	m	t	w	t	f	s
			1	2	3	4
5	6	7	8	9	10	11
12	13	14	15	16	17	18
19	20	21	22	23	24	25
26	27	28	29	30	31	

january

Norwegian author and explorer Helge Ingstad b. 1899

monday
30 364

School

Author and home economist Mary Virginia Terhune b. 1831

tuesday
31 365

Ross

NEW YEAR'S DAY
Betsy Ross b. 1752

wednesday
1 1

BANK HOLIDAY (SCOTLAND)
M. Carey Thomas, pioneer of women's higher education, b. 1857

thursday
● 2 2

Lucretia Coffin Mott, abolitionist and woman's rights leader, b. 1793

Soccer 10³⁰ pm

friday
3 3

Selena Butler, advocate-leader of interracial cooperation, b. 1872

Ross?

saturday
4 4

Olympia Brown, pacifist and Universalist minister, b. 1835

sunday
5 5

International Holidays

Following is a list of major (bank-closing) holidays for some countries around the world. Holidays for the U.S., U.K., and Canada appear on this calendar's grid pages, as well as major Jewish holidays. We apologize if we have omitted countries of interest to you, but space constraints limit our selection.

Australia

1 January	New Year's Day
26 January	Australia Day
11 March	Labor Day (Victoria)
29 March	Good Friday
1 April	Easter Monday
25 April	Anzac Day
10 June	Queen's Birthday
5 August	Bank Holiday (New South Wales)
7 October	Labor Day (New South Wales)
5 November	Melbourne Cup Day (Victoria)
25 December	Christmas
26 December	Boxing Day

Brazil

1 January	New Year's Day
20 January	Foundation Day (Rio de Janeiro)
25 January	Foundation Day (São Paulo)
11–12 February	Carnival
29 March	Good Friday
21 April	Independence Hero Tiradentes
1 May	Labor Day
30 May	Corpus Christi
9 July	Constitution Day (São Paulo)
7 September	Independence Day
12 October	Religious Day
2 November	All Souls' Day
15 November	Proclamation of the Republic
25 December	Christmas

Chile

1 January	New Year's Day
29 March	Good Friday
30 March	Holy Saturday
1 May	Labor Day
21 May	Navy Day
30 May	Corpus Christi
29 June	Sts. Peter and Paul
15 August	Assumption Day
2 September	National Unity Day
18 September	Independence Day
19 September	Army Day
12 October	Hispanity Day
1 November	All Saints' Day

8 December	Immaculate Conception
25 December	Christmas
31 December	Bank Holiday

China (see also Hong Kong)

1 January	New Year's Day
12–14 February	Lunar New Year
1–3 May	Labor Day Holiday
1–3 October	National Holiday

Denmark

1 January	New Year's Day
28 March	Holy Thursday
29 March	Good Friday
1 April	Easter Monday
26 April	General Prayer Day
9 May	Ascension Day
20 May	Whitmonday
5 June	Constitution Day
24 December	Christmas Eve
25 December	Christmas
26 December	Boxing Day

France

1 January	New Year's Day
1 April	Easter Monday
1 May	Labor Day
8 May	Armistice Day
9 May	Ascension Day
20 May	Whitmonday
14 July	Bastille Day
15 August	Assumption Day
1 November	All Saints' Day
11 November	Armistice Day
25 December	Christmas

Germany

1 January	New Year's Day
29 March	Good Friday
1 April	Easter Monday
1 May	Labor Day
9 May	Ascension Day
20 May	Whitmonday
30 May	Corpus Christi
3 October	National Day
24 December	Christmas Eve
25 December	Christmas
26 December	Boxing Day
31 December	New Year's Eve

Hong Kong

1 January	New Year's Day
12–14 February	Lunar New Year
29 March	Good Friday
30 March	Holy Saturday
1 April	Easter Monday
5 April	Ching Ming Festival
1 May	Labor Day
20 May	Buddha's Birthday
15 June	Tuen Ng Day
1 July	SAR Establishment Day
23 September	Mid-Autumn Festival
1 October	National Holiday
14 October	Chung Yeung Day
25–26 Dec.	Christmas Holiday

India

26 January	Republic Day
23 February	Bakr-Id
24 March	Muharram
29 March	Good Friday
1 April	Yearly bank closing
14 April	Babasaheb Ambedkar's Birthday
1 May	Maharashtra Day (or May Day)
24 May	Id-e-Milad (Muhammad's Birthday)
27 May	Buddha Purnima
15 August	Independence Day
21 August	Parsi New Year
30 September	Half-yearly bank closing
2 October	Mahatma Gandhi's Birthday
5 November	Diwali (Laxmipujan)
7 December	Id-ul-Fitar
25 December	Christmas Day (additional holidays to be declared)

Israel

26 February	Purim (Tel Aviv)
27 February	Purim
28 March	First day of Pesach
3 April	Last day of Pesach
17 April	National Independence Day
17 May	Shavuot
18 July	Fast of the Ninth of Av
7–8 September	Rosh Hashanah
15–16 Sept.	Yom Kippur
21 September	First day of Sukkot
28 September	Shemini Atzeret

International Holidays

Italy

1 January	New Year's Day
6 January	Epiphany
1 April	Easter Monday
25 April	Liberation Day
1 May	Labor Day
15 August	Assumption Day
1 November	All Saints' Day
8 December	Immaculate Conception
25 December	Christmas
26 December	St. Stephen's Day

Japan

1–3 January	New Year's Holiday
14 January	Coming of Age Day
11 February	National Foundation Day
21 March	Vernal Equinox
29 April	Greenery Day
3 May	Constitution Day
4 May	National Holiday
6 May	Children's Day
20 July	Ocean Day
16 September	Respect for the Aged Day
23 September	Autumnal Equinox
14 October	Health and Sports Day
4 November	Culture Day
23 November	Labor Thanksgiving Day
23 December	Emperor's Birthday
31 December	New Year's Eve

Kenya

1 January	New Year's Day
29 March	Good Friday
1 April	Easter Monday
1 May	Labor Day
1 June	Madaraka Day
10 October	Moi Day
21 October	Kenyatta Day
6 December	Eid-al-Fitr
12 December	Jamhuri Day
25 December	Christmas
26 December	Boxing Day

Korea

1 January	New Year's Day
11–13 February	Lunar New Year
1 March	Independence Movement Day
5 April	Arbor Day
1 May	Labor Day
5 May	Children's Day
19 May	Buddha's Birthday
6 June	Memorial Day
17 July	Constitution Day
15 August	Liberation Day
20–22 Sept.	Harvest Moon Festival
3 October	National Foundation Day
25 December	Christmas

Malaysia

1 January	New Year's Day
1 February	Federal Territory Day
12–13 February	Lunar New Year
23 February	Hari Raya Haji
15 March	First day of Muharram
1 May	Labor Day
24 May	Prophet Muhammad's Birthday
27 May	Wesak Day
1 June	Yang DiPertuan Agong's Birthday
31 August	National Day
5 November	Deepavali
6–7 December	Hari Raya Puasa
25 December	Christmas

Mexico

1 January	New Year's Day
5 February	Constitution Day
21 March	Juárez's Birthday
28 March	Holy Thursday
29 March	Good Friday
30 March	Holy Saturday
1 May	Labor Day
5 May	Battle of Puebla
1 September	Government's Report
16 September	Independence Day
20 November	Revolution Day
12 December	Our Lady of Guadalupe
25 December	Christmas

New Zealand

1–2 January	New Year's Holiday
21 January	Wellington Provincial Anniversary
28 January	Auckland Provincial Anniversary
6 February	Waitangi Day
29 March	Good Friday
1 April	Easter Monday
25 April	Anzac Day
3 June	Queen's Birthday
28 October	Labor Day
25 December	Christmas
26 December	Boxing Day

Saudi Arabia

22–26 February	Eid-al-Adha
5–7 December	Eid-al-Fitr
(dates subject to adjustment)	

Singapore

1 January	New Year's Day
12–13 February	Lunar New Year
23 February	Hari Raya Haji
29 March	Good Friday
1 May	Labor Day
27 May	Wesak Day
9 August	National Day
5 November	Deepavali
6 December	Hari Raya Puasa
25 December	Christmas

South Africa

1 January	New Year's Day
21 March	Human Rights Day
29 March	Good Friday
1 April	Family Day
27 April	Freedom Day
1 May	Workers' Day
17 June	Youth Day
9 August	National Women's Day
24 September	Heritage Day
16 December	Day of Reconciliation
25 December	Christmas
26 December	Day of Goodwill

Spain

1 January	New Year's Day
6 January	Epiphany
28 March	Holy Thursday
29 March	Good Friday
1 May	Labor Day
2 May	Independence Day
15 May	San Isidro's Day
15 August	Assumption Day
12 October	Hispanity Day
1 November	All Saints' Day
9 November	Our Lady of Almudena
6 December	Constitution Day
8 December	Immaculate Conception
25 December	Christmas

Switzerland

1 January	New Year's Day
2 January	Berchtoldstag
29 March	Good Friday
1 April	Easter Monday
1 May	Labor Day
9 May	Ascension Day
20 May	Whitmonday
1 August	National Day
25 December	Christmas
26 December	St. Stephen's Day
31 December	New Year's Eve

INFORMATION COURTESY OF WWW.GOODBUSINESSDAY.COM

2003

january

s	m	t	w	t	f	s
			1	2	3	4
5	6	7	8	9	10	11
12	13	14	15	16	17	18
19	20	21	22	23	24	25
26	27	28	29	30	31	

february

s	m	t	w	t	f	s
						1
2	3	4	5	6	7	8
9	10	11	12	13	14	15
16	17	18	19	20	21	22
23	24	25	26	27	28	

march

s	m	t	w	t	f	s
						1
2	3	4	5	6	7	8
9	10	11	12	13	14	15
16	17	18	19	20	21	22
23	24	25	26	27	28	29
30	31					

april

s	m	t	w	t	f	s
		1	2	3	4	5
6	7	8	9	10	11	12
13	14	15	16	17	18	19
20	21	22	23	24	25	26
27	28	29	30			

may

s	m	t	w	t	f	s
				1	2	3
4	5	6	7	8	9	10
11	12	13	14	15	16	17
18	19	20	21	22	23	24
25	26	27	28	29	30	31

june

s	m	t	w	t	f	s
1	2	3	4	5	6	7
8	9	10	11	12	13	14
15	16	17	18	19	20	21
22	23	24	25	26	27	28
29	30					

july

s	m	t	w	t	f	s
		1	2	3	4	5
6	7	8	9	10	11	12
13	14	15	16	17	18	19
20	21	22	23	24	25	26
27	28	29	30	31		

august

s	m	t	w	t	f	s
					1	2
3	4	5	6	7	8	9
10	11	12	13	14	15	16
17	18	19	20	21	22	23
24	25	26	27	28	29	30
31						

september

s	m	t	w	t	f	s
	1	2	3	4	5	6
7	8	9	10	11	12	13
14	15	16	17	18	19	20
21	22	23	24	25	26	27
28	29	30				

october

s	m	t	w	t	f	s
			1	2	3	4
5	6	7	8	9	10	11
12	13	14	15	16	17	18
19	20	21	22	23	24	25
26	27	28	29	30	31	

november

s	m	t	w	t	f	s
						1
2	3	4	5	6	7	8
9	10	11	12	13	14	15
16	17	18	19	20	21	22
23	24	25	26	27	28	29
30						

december

s	m	t	w	t	f	s
	1	2	3	4	5	6
7	8	9	10	11	12	13
14	15	16	17	18	19	20
21	22	23	24	25	26	27
28	29	30	31			